PRESENT DISCONTENTS

American Politics in the Very Late Twentieth Century

BYRON E. SHAFER

with

Joel H. Silbey

Michael Barone

Charles O. Jones

Alan Ehrenhalt

Edward G. Carmines

Geoffrey C. Layman

Thomas B. Edsall

Chatham House Publishers, Inc.
Chatham, New Jersey

PRESENT DISCONTENTS:
American Politics in the Very Late Twentieth Century

Chatham House Publishers, Inc.
Post Office Box One
Chatham, New Jersey 07928

Publisher: Edward Artinian
Cover design: Antler and Baldwin Design Group, Inc.
Production supervisor: Katharine Miller
Composition: Bang, Motley, Olufsen
Printing and binding: R.R. Donnelley and Sons Company

Library of Congress Cataloging-in-Publication Data

Present discontents : American politics in the very late twentieth
century / edited by Byron E. Shafer.
    p.   cm.
    Includes bibliographical references and index.
    ISBN 1-56643-050-X (pbk.)
    1. United States—Politics and government.   I. Shafer, Byron E.
JK271.A37   1997
320.973—dc20
                                                    96-45775
                                                        CIP

Printed in the United States of America
    10   9   8   7   6   5   4   3   2   1

Contents

Preface

THIS BOOK GREW out of two series of public lectures at Oxford University, series concerned with interpreting American politics in the very late twentieth century. Revised versions of those lectures constitute the chapters that follow. The postwar period—the years between the end of World War II and the present—was the focus for all speakers, and all were concerned with the evolution of American politics across that period. Otherwise, each began with a single and specific aspect of that politics: parties, society, institutions, culture, issues, agendas, and coalitions.

Those who already know these authors—Messrs. Barone, Carmines and Layman, Edsall, Ehrenhalt, Jones, Shafer, and Silbey—will know that they are distinguished by being macro interpreters of American politics; there are no political miniaturists here. Those who know them will also know that each has a distinctive perspective, even a distinctive voice; these too are very much in evidence. Those who do not yet know some or all of these authors are about to discover that they can organize and interpret a broad sweep of American politics in a concise, lively, and *forceful* way.

Some readers will surely be struck by the differences among them, in the conclusions they draw from their particular pieces of the puzzle. They do differ in evaluating present discontents, not only in the degree of alarm which they regard as appropriate, but in the degree to which they view current problems in American politics as unprecedented in an evolutionary sense or as merely the current incarnations of long-running (and recurrent) tensions. The view of the editor, however—my view—is that what is equally striking about all these analyses is the underlying similarity of the interpretations, and hence of empirical diagnoses. Beginning with separable but very major pieces of the puzzle, they are, one after another, led ultimately toward remarkably parallel analyses.

Or so it seemed to me, though that is inevitably a matter for each reader to judge individually. Large and rumbustious initial audiences at Oxford were certainly prepared to argue. Happily, Ed Artinian and his staff at Chatham House were not, at least about the process of converting these essays into a book. None of this would have been possible without the support of the Andrew W. Mellon Fund, and thus ultimately of the Andrew W. Mellon Foundation, or without the encouragement of its committee at Oxford—Nigel Bowles, Desmond King, John Rowett, Alan Ware, and Laurence Whitehead. I hope they draw some satisfaction from the product. The result, in any case, is present—without discontent—in the seven chapters that follow.

PARTIES

JOEL H. SILBEY

Foundation Stones of Present Discontents:
The American Political Nation,
1776–1945

I T IS NO SECRET that we live in troubled political times. Everywhere in the world, in nations with long and settled traditions of popular government and in those struggling to create new institutions of governance or to redefine themselves in the aftermath of the Cold War, there is widespread cynicism at the end of the twentieth century: enormous negativism toward existing political systems; an often frenetic impatience with, and frustration about, the failure of leadership; apparent deviousness by politicians at every level—"I won't be voting," *The Guardian* quoted an apparently not untypical Londoner just before England's local elections in early 1994, "they're all bleeding liars, ain't they?"—and the ultimate inability of our political institutions to deal with the daunting range of critical problems that affect us all.[1]

Much of the available evidence suggests that such negativism is not misplaced. In this line of argument, the world has indeed entered an age of stark political decline, not only in the macrocosmic economic and military sense of overstretch, the consequent rise and fall that Paul Kennedy has presented, but also in the current level of leadership skills and in the ability of many nations, settled systems and otherwise, to deal competently with the derivative and ordinary political affairs that occur everywhere on a day-to-day basis. Decline into ineptitude appears to define our lot.[2]

The United States has not been immune from these unhappy currents. Its political system has been unusually durable and, as many Americans like to believe, can be viewed as having evolved over time toward ever-higher levels of democratic achievement and ever-better ways and means of accomplishing the national purpose. The nation's political system, after all, reaches across a broader landscape than it ever has before, is undeniably more democratic than in earlier times, and remains an important focus for those seeking to get their way in a sprawling and complex society. But for a nation that has prided itself on its political stability, its ability to get things done, and its success in incorporating significant changes without great fuss, Americans are now undergoing a particularly unsettling version (for them) of the declinist complaint. The nation's political commentary is awash in unremitting, harsh, and despairing assertions about institutional and leadership inadequacies; about sleaze, corruption, scandal, and selfishness; about systemic incoherence, unresponsiveness, drift, and ineffectiveness.[3]

Americans' persistent focus on political morality has become a vehicle for relentlessly denouncing all politicians and the political process itself. Expressions of resentment and anger at the way that the system operates (or fails to operate) have become cacophonous—and not only among the friends of Ross Perot. Current media frenzy focuses all but exclusively on highly negative and sour reporting of the failures, deceptions, and unrequited malignant conduct of our political leaders. Savage reports of personal and institutional failures are the everyday stuff of even the most sober commentary. Elections are swamps of chaotic and confusing name-calling. They neither improve matters nor clarify what we are about—they do not "solve" anything. In fact, a growing body of opinion suggests that America's normal political fare means little, except to reveal all too many moments of extreme manipulative and deceptive practices.[4]

All of this negativism has had an impact. In an era in which individual character failures constitute the primary emphasis of American political discourse and have become a major determinant of voter choice, whatever the issues argued and the policies articulated, popular political behavior has become highly volatile and itself unusually angry and negative. Few presidents survive for very long; all officeholders have become suspect—when they are not despised. Polls indicate deep distrust of our leaders and frustration about the system they manage. "The sad truth is," two professional analysts of polling data conclude, "that we have come to expect lies, distortion, and deception as everyday occurrences in politics." The professional politician has become very damaged goods—the epithet "Washington insider" is a redundant accusation—the survival of each threatened by popular protests and the future of all threatened by the passage of unprecedented reform legislation. At the same time, the policymaking apparatus that they inhabit is viewed as totally ineffective, except when it comes to confirming or extending the perks enjoyed by legislators and bureaucrats.[5]

Most troubling of all is that this miserable state of affairs is no longer viewed in the media or in the public at large as temporary and correctable, when matters inevitably return to an even keel, as they have always done in the past. As threatening as anything can be to the current health of American democratic politics is that much of the critical dialogue about it strongly articulates the notion not only of a major but of a permanent governability crisis, dominated by unremitting systemic dysfunction, deterioration, and irreversible, terminal decline. "It is now close to a universal belief among Americans," Walter Dean Burnham has written, "that time is not on our side," in confronting and successfully dealing with the problems that beset us and demand a political response.[6]

Time was once always on their side—or so Americans liked to believe. When it no longer is, or is believed not to be, one can only conclude that there is something deeply amiss in the American political system, an extraordinary loss of public confidence in it and in any commitment to be patient and tolerant of its difficulties, to await better days. Everywhere, there is the corrosive reality of failure and rejection. As the Brookings Institution scholar Thomas Mann suggested after the presidential election of 1992, there is little but "anger and contempt" in the United States "for the political process. . . . What is a normal political process is seen as somehow tainted and demeaning," not to mention cumbersome, unresponsive, ineffective, and ultimately debilitating. In fine, "the American people no longer believe in their government."[7]

There are some irreducible facts within all of this negativism, whatever the levels of hyperbole and exaggeration present in its expression. A great deal has changed on the American political landscape, and much of what now occurs there cannot be defined as a positive good. The American government has never been particularly nimble in its activities, but as the range of current expectations and policy entitlements has grown, all but exponentially, there has been a steep decline in the system's governing and socializing capabilities, even from the less-than-ideal situation of previous eras. But why has that happened at this moment in our history? Is such dysfunction inevitable, given massive technological changes and the exhaustion of reigning ideologies such as liberalism, which have for so long given shape and understanding to our political experience, or is it the result of the extraordinary power of other disruptive social and economic elements now intruding into the political realm? Unfortunately, we do not really know, although much scholarly speculation exists, not to mention a great deal of media analysis, much of it unfortunately confusing and contradictory.[8]

There is also a counterpart level of complacency among some observers, who suggest that there is less here than meets the eye—that popular and media negativism has missed the critical (and reassuring) point that there are always such moments of difficulty in political life, moments that are usually followed by the system righting itself in a rhythmic pattern of restoration. "Cheer up," *The Economist*'s American correspondent suggested in early 1994, "things are really not that bad." Some scholars agree with that proposition and point out that important and depressing political transformations have occurred before but that there has always been a self-regulating mechanism present to restore the system to its normal keel after a period of disruption and tension. We should, in this view, step back, relax a little, take a long perspective, and await the impact of the system's inherent restorative forces.[9]

I do not agree. The evidence we have suggests that such restorative forces no longer exist in the way they once did. If there has been a rhythmic pattern to American politics involving, among other qualities, powerful mechanisms that operate to return the political nation to some efficacious balance even after the most disheartening episodes, it is no longer obviously present on the American landscape. I have argued elsewhere, for example, that to see our present political situation as part of a familiar cyclical pattern encompassing a sixth party system in a recurring line stretching back to 1789—each similar in style and basic organization, each defined, energized, and renewed by periodic electoral realignments, each eventually bringing the system back to a basic, sustainable norm of conflict, management, and reasonable accomplishment—inadequately locates our present situation.[10]

The reason for that conceptual inadequacy is that our prevailing notion of a cyclical pattern of change and restoration in American political history, driven by partisan and voting realignments, is too time-bound to be useful for the analytic purposes to which scholars have put it. The conditions that underlay recurring party systems and allowed for periodic shifts in their nature, while retaining the basic stability of the system as a whole, existed for only part of our history. Most critically, they no longer do. Instead, and centrally, I believe Robert Dahl's formulation, that Americans now live in new and very unfamiliar territory, is correct. We inhabit a distinct moment unlike any previous one in our history, in which the central thrust of political life is very different from what has gone before, a moment that is, distinctively, largely disintegrative in nature. As Dahl suggests, the two dominating aspects of America's current political order are that "government policies are made in response to a greater number and variety of conflicting and substantially autonomous interest groups," and at the same time "political institutions for encouraging these conflicting interest groups to negotiate ... in search of mutually beneficial policies, are ... weaker than before."[11] The current order cannot be viewed as simply the recurrence, once again, of a periodic disruption that always challenges but does not overthrow the nation's basic political stability. As a result, our understanding of where we came from and what we now are politically has to be reconsidered through different lenses than that of the party-systems framework with its implicit assumptions of patterned restoration and regeneration.

American Political Eras and the Power of History

There is a second point to be made about these matters. Many scholars, as well as most popular commentators, emphasize relatively recent events as the source of our current dismaying political condition. Most of them focus, in particular, on the massive disintegrative impulses of the 1960s, a decade that did not see the expected electoral realignment supposedly due then, but in which much about American political life was transformed, and not for the better. "This book ... is about a change in American society and behavior over the past thirty or so years," Jonathan Rauch has written at the outset of his angry analysis of our current situation, "which is compromising our ability to govern ourselves and to solve common problems." Other events, such as the antiwar uproar, the repeated iniquities of our political leadership, the challenges to most "establishment" institutions, and the rising power of television to affect and change people's perspectives about the political world, all made important additional contributions to shaping our current political nation and the polarizing and coarsening of our civic culture.[12]

There is a great deal of truth in notions about the contribution of events of the 1960s to the transformation of our political capabilities since. But a primary focus on that decade does not, it seems to me, go far enough into the previous patterns, structures, and shape of the political nation and the directions that it took at earlier moments in our history. The dynamics undergirding current political angst in the United States are much more long run than the focus on a single recent decade allows. The events of the 1960s had an impact on an environment that already was in the throes of transformative political changes, the result of a basic long-term metamorphosis of institutions, attitudes, and, ultimately, behavior—culminating in, and marked by, a shift in institutional structures and cultural perspectives of truly revolutionary dimensions.

To bring these criticisms to a point, I suggest that to comprehend what is now happening on the national political landscape, analysis has to begin by employing a different organizing concept, that of distinct political eras, as the basic structuring dimension of American political history. Whatever cyclical elements have been present to shape and set boundaries amid a recurrent pulse to American political history, they were not alone. Other elements existed as well, elements that shaped the system institutionally, first in an evolutionary and then in a degenerative pattern. The notion of political eras catches these alternative impulses and provides, I suggest, a quite useful and much more informative way of describing and understanding why we have reached our current problematic political state.[13]

Much happened in American politics between the founding of the nation and the end of World War II in 1945. On the surface, much of the political nation looks remarkably stable. It has not been. Beneath the same regular contests for office, the annual meetings of Congress and state legislatures, which do occur over and over, along with the other normal activities connected with national political development, the ways in which Americans dealt with their political needs have changed dramatically over two hundred years. As a result, there were distinctive frameworks organizing what happened on the landscape, these frameworks forming into four distinct political eras, and the period since 1945 has been only the most recent among them (see table 1.1). Each of these eras succeeded and built upon what was already on the ground. But each contained elements that were distinct from all of the others, with different ways of doing business and different centers of gravity, and each had quite different capabilities—and reputations —as a result.

A full elaboration of all the elements constituting each of the nation's political eras would range from the notions about politics held

TABLE 1.1

AMERICAN POLITICAL ERAS

Era	Description	Dates
1	Prepartisan/prealignment	1789–1838
2	Partisan/alignment-realignment	1838–93
3	Postpartisan/realignment-dealignment	1893–1945
4	Nonpartisan/postalignment	1945–90 and beyond

by both political leaders and the general population at different moments, up to and including the power and reach of government itself. Such an elaboration would include the process by which policy was made; the extent and nature of popular involvement in formal political activity; and the role played by particular institutions, most especially national political parties, in organizing the system, articulating what was at stake in each era, bringing Americans into contact with their government and the rest of the political process, and influencing how they acted to achieve their particular ends.[14]

Parties have existed in America since the 1790s. But their function and importance have constantly varied, as dictated by needs and pressures in the political nation at different moments as well as by the shifting balances among particular ideological constructs that existed—ideological constructs that continually debated the appropriateness of such institutions.[15] The nature of the issues defining the political world, and identifying what was at stake at a given moment, were usually readily agreed upon. But how political participants were to accomplish their purposes has always been vigorously contested, in particular over the correct balance between distinct institutional ways of dealing with political matters, that is, over the role played by political parties in shaping and influencing individual and aggregate behavior. The way that this contest played out is, to reiterate my main perspective, the key to understanding not only the nature of our past politics but why the nation's political present is what it has become.

All of which brings me, at last, to the point of this essay. A consideration of the nature of our current political landscape will be undertaken by those who follow me in this collection. My intention is to set the stage for their analysis by locating and describing the foundations on which our present situation rests, since, given what I have said, such an examination provides the necessary long-range context for understanding the roots and nature of our political transformation. My argument is that however much recent socioeconomic conditions, ideological shifts, and particular events in the 1960s contributed to it, America's current political malaise is rooted first and foremost in the collapse, beginning with the onset of the third political era at the end of the nineteenth century, of the partisan institutional framework critically and absolutely necessary for the effective operation and health of the American political world.[16]

From its beginnings in the colonial era, the American scene was contentious and grew steadily more so. The problem of disciplining and directing a political nation subject to roiling fragmentation and unremitting factional and real conflicts preoccupied a great many American political leaders from the outset, beginning with James Madison and continuing through Martin Van Buren, John C. Calhoun, and, later, a range of Progressive reformers, academics, and outside observers right into the present. If the United States was destined to be the scene of persistent social, economic, and political conflict, these needed to be managed effectively. But how was this to be done; how far would any attempts to bring order extend throughout the political community? What impact would such management have on the autonomy of individuals and communities to go their own way or on the particular needs of specific groups, the security of different interests, classes, and sections?[17]

The answers to these questions were always elusive because they were fiercely contested. There was a persistent and powerful disagreement about them, in fact about the arts of political management generally. This disagreement has materially contributed to the framing of America's political experience, divided it, and helped shape it into the distinctive eras the nation has had. Most pertinently, the contestation over how to organize politics led to the further bifurcation of America's political development, a bifurcation that involved two critical transformative changes in direction in the way that we organize and articulate the political world.

The first of these changes occurred between the first and second political eras, the second occurred between the second era and the two eras that have followed. The first transformation, growing out of the dangerously divisive turmoil of the post-1815 decades, led to the establishment of America's only partisan dominant era, which existed between the late 1830s and the early 1890s.[18] The second of these critical shifts in direction, associated with the Populist-Progressive years, initiated a long secular trend that powerfully challenged, and then overthrew, the deeply rooted partisan way of organizing and articulating American political life.

In that long secular trend lie the roots of our current situation, though a number of other things filtered into it as well. Our experience during the moments of great reformist energy between the 1890s and the 1940s, encompassing America's third political era—beginning with the Populist uprising of the 1890s and the Progressive assault on partisan politics and followed by the New Deal and then the expansion of government during World War II—all had in common an extraordinary assault on the ability of Americans to make their politics coherent and functional through the established partisan institutions that had traditionally performed those tasks.[19]

These challenges, followed in turn by the massive uproar against normal politics that we associate with the 1960s, accumulated and synthesized into a very different political situation from what had earlier been present and created the particular landscape on which subsequent forces operated. The fourth American political era, beginning

9

around 1945, encompasses the activities of the 1960s and continues to the present day. By extending our analysis longitudinally, therefore, that is, by examining the nation's current situation through a lens focused on particular situations and definitional norms occurring farther back in our past than has usually been the case among scholars, we will get a better purchase on current phenomena than anyone has to date.

"Abhorrence of Party Spirit"

The first political era under the Constitution lasted from 1789 to the late 1830s. Originating in the transatlantic republican tradition, the colonial experience, and the confrontation with the mother country, it contained all the elements that would continue to shape the unfolding of the American political experience thereafter. His late majesty King George III has much to answer for—not only for the colonial claim of oppression at his hands but because, in opposition to what Americans believed about his power, policies, and perceived transgressions, a particular design of government emerged in the United States that formally splintered authority in order to limit and bifurcate central power. American ideology and political history dictated such a course. However much centralists wanted to shape the American system in a particular direction, the nation's experience and reigning ideology dictated severe limits to their efforts. The attempts of the founding fathers to increase the power of the center constantly ran up against the need to divide and separate the powers placed there and to retain a great deal of residual local and state power able to challenge, check, and balance the authority of the center.[20]

Whatever its improvement over the existing institutional framework in the new republic, a constitution that weakened authority by cutting it up into many parts made a coherent and purposive government all but impossible to construct. Yet such partitioned government framed a political nation where a great deal always seemed to be at stake in elections and in the activities of the state and national governments. An enduring reality of American life was that whatever consensual processes existed in the society from the beginning, there was also persistent conflict—conflict fostered and shaped by significant differences in ethnoreligious, class, regional, and economic perspectives, along with the demands and goals that flowed unremittingly from those differences.

American political practice, therefore, as many recognized from the outset, called for effective organization across a broad landscape, organization that crossed state lines and encompassed all of the different locations and levels of government that existed in the new nation. But except for a number of brief moments at the outset, leaders in this first political era found no way to construct such organization, no sustained answer to the problem of contentious factions and divided authority. Political activity continued to be fractured, disconnected, and often chaotic. Although national parties appeared in the 1790s and party labels identified the contestants vying for power, their reach, influence, and ultimate importance remained shallow and circumscribed. There was never a fully realized party system on the ground in this era. As I have written elsewhere, "there was always an intermittent, ad hoc, impermanent quality about the Federalists and Republicans, often a casual, or, conversely, a quite hostile attitude toward them."[21]

This was largely because, as a generation of historians have told us, the defining impulse of the first political era was its continuing roots not only in the experience associated with Britain in the eighteenth century but also in the reigning republican political philosophy of the transatlantic community, a philosophy built around a deep suspicion and fear of the misuse of power both by despots and by conniving, manipulative politicians, and one that stretched even farther back in time beyond the revolution to the very sources of Anglo-American political perspectives in the Renaissance. That ideology made it clear that America's liberty was perpetually menaced by power. Republicanism's fragility could thus be protected not only by the diffusion of power as enshrined in the constitutional arrangements constructed in 1787 but by the careful avoidance subsequently of artful and threatening political combinations within the society. "Governments, and especially republican governments," Lacey Ford has recently summarized the prevailing perspective, "had to be designed and constructed with sufficient safeguards to prevent both the tyranny of one group of citizens over another and the tyranny of the government over the citizenry."[22]

Political parties (or *factions,* a term then used interchangeably) were particularly threatening to republicanism's survival. As Henry Jones Ford has written, "the old Whig abhorrence of party spirit raged in the bosoms of the fathers." Parties were corrupting, conspiratorial, scheming organizations, interested only in the promotion of their own parochial concerns, dangerous threats in their outlook and behavior to a stable republican order, promoting internal conflicts and abetting corrupt factions intent solely on selfish behavior, instead of promoting the general good. As a result, many American political leaders of the founding generation (and afterward) were quick to condemn what one of them called "the bigotry of party." Such organizations did not belong in the new republic.[23]

But the problem of vigorously contesting factions, always at war with each other across a chaotic landscape, provoked a major revolution in American politics at the end of the first half-century under the Constitution: the extraordinary rise of national political parties to become the central institutions of national life. These parties did not develop out of anyone's master plan but out of an increasingly recognized need to elaborate a political process that stressed the skills of management, to find a way in a highly pluralistic society to mediate among and conciliate conflicting groups. The search for the skills of aggregation, in a political culture with immense potential for factionalization and disorder, preoccupied political leaders throughout the Union after the end of the War of 1812. Such fragmenting and threatening episodes as the Hartford Convention, the controversy over the admission of Missouri as a slave state, and the four-candidate tumult in the presidential election of 1824 more than convinced them of the urgent need to find some new, more certain means of organizing, managing, and directing political activity.[24]

Parties "Never Yet Injured Any Free Country"

Unlike their predecessors, the political leaders of the 1820s and 1830s accepted that constant political conflict was inevitable, that real differences over public policy were a permanent fact of American life, and that, therefore, cooperation among like-minded groups was necessary, normal, and proper. The emergence of popular politics by the 1830s also demanded more developed and intricate institutions of political activity. National political parties, in the eyes of this new generation of founders, provided a logical and effective solution to the problem of management, aggregation, and cooperation. Churchill Cambreleng, Martin Van Buren's close ally, forcefully argued in a speech in Congress in 1826 that such parties were "indispensable to every administration [and] ... essential to the existence of our institutions; and if [they are] ... an evil [they are one] we must endure, for the preservation of our civil liberty." But parties, he continued, "never yet injured any free country.... The conflict of parties is a noble conflict—of mind to mind, genius to genius."[25]

Cambreleng's revisionist arguments were relentlessly repeated throughout the nation in the 1820s and 1830s. They had rarely been heard with such force and intensity before, and at first they were bitterly resisted; they did not immediately sweep the field. Nevertheless, the sense that existing political institutions were not up to the task was increasingly widespread and influential. The growth of the nation geographically, along with the widening democratic impulses present—particularly the expansion of the electorate, ultimately to incorporate most adult white males by 1840—was a further prod toward order, direction, and management. The positive argument for national parties united with pragmatic considerations to bring success to this revolution and the widespread adoption of partisan norms, despite some continued heartburn and hesitation.[26]

The second American political era as it emerged by the late 1830s, therefore, had a much different character than its predecessor, with different organizational and behavioral norms from the immediate past, as well as a sharp rejection of a powerful intellectual tradition of nonpartisanship. Parties justified their acceptance quickly. They largely brought factional chaos under control, albeit they found many bumps in the road as they did so. Internal party disputes were a constant, for instance, but were usually smoothed over as the parties unified into disciplined armies to confront their common enemy.[27]

They did more than that. Parties in the nineteenth century socialized people into acting together on behalf of ideas, commitments, and policies that were relentlessly hammered into the public consciousness. Parties were the fulcrum of whatever policymaking occurred, and their leaders sought, always, to banish confusion, fragmentation, and frustrations (except to the other party). They usually succeeded. Whatever made American voters distinct—their class identities, ideology, religion and ethnicity, worldviews, region, and/or some specific interest—such distinctive identities were subsumed within the aggregating compass of the two-party system. Parties allowed the United States to engage in a raucous and uncouth politics, populist in tone and somewhat egalitarian in intent. There was always a policy component to the parties. Each pushed forward clusters of ideas, values, outlooks, and demands that differed from one another. Whigs and Democrats articulated the policy and value differences present in vigorous fashion and successfully clarified what was at stake in the nation's political conflicts.

Finally, in addition to providing mediating, disciplining, and expressive functions, as important as each was, parties established an intimate relationship between the voters and the political process, between individual persons and the leadership at every level. In a society devoid of large-scale and intrusive institutions of national authority, parties brought people and their political system together. The whole range of partisan institutions, from the regular meeting of local conventions to the frequent campaign rallies to the hoopla of getting out the vote on election day, all deeply embedded politics—what was at stake and what one should do—into the voters' (and others') minds, emotions, and appetites. Participation in campaign rallies and election activities was widespread and was never limited solely to those eligible to vote. An interactive relationship between voters, their families, and the political world prevailed as a result. Partisan campaigns loudly aroused the faithful, identified what was at stake, and brought everyone together in crusading armies against a common foe.

As a result of these activities, parties successfully mobilized an expanding electorate. Turnout at the polls on succeeding election days soared to heights rarely seen before, and never with such constancy and regularity. And voters were powerfully anchored in their party loyalties in election after election. Leaders paid attention to keeping them there. To all, leaders and followers alike, parties were central to what they were about in politics, and those politics counted. A citizen's party was seen, throughout the political nation, to be, in the words of a Whig congressman, "the salt of the nation. It establishes watchfulness and wholesome guardianship over the institutions of our country; it checks and restrains the reckless ambition of those in office and never fails to expose the nonfeasance, misfeasance, or malfeasance of those in power." Each political party, a Democratic colleague summed up, allowed "the people to declare their will in practical form."[28]

By the early 1840s, political parties became the mainstay of a political nation that clearly needed them but had once denounced them. As the first successful aggregating institutions on the American scene, they reached widely and dominated everything, commanding unprecedented political power, unlike anything that had existed before or would come later. Politics, elections, and policies were about party, not about individuals, about large-scale perspectives across different groups, not about narrow parochial interests. Party connections, loyalty, and discipline proved critical during the moments of policymaking that did occur under Presidents Lincoln, Polk, and, briefly, Zachary Taylor. And their absence severely hampered Presidents John Tyler and Andrew Johnson. A nationwide and competitive two-party system was impressive in its reach, importance, and role; had remarkable force and staying power within a loudly expressive political culture; and was marked, most of all, by an intense popular commitment to parties and their ways. The startling conquest of the previously powerful cultural and ideological resistance to parties, and their successful establishment in the role they had, was an extraordinary event, the first major transformative change in the nature of the American political nation under the Constitution.[29]

For the rest of the nineteenth century, political parties continued to organize and manage the socioeconomic dynamics defining the American scene. A set of contrarian fragmenting forces, sectional and reformist, always existed. These cut across the cleavages that parties embodied and the behaviors that parties instilled in the political world, repeatedly challenging them as inadequate and misdirected. These challengers were contained for much of the period, however, by the countervailing force of partisan linkage and socialization. Challengers discovered that they had to play by the partisan rules of the game. Provocatively and tellingly, when sectional forces grew in force on the scene in the 1850s and after, much of their growth was through the organization of a political party to harness and propel the impulse.[30]

To be sure, the parties were altered and transformed by shifts in their basic voting support in the electoral realignments of the 1850s and later. The increase of ideological intensity along sectional lines shook the political nation severely. In the aftermath, politics and parties contained a much more significant sectional component to them than had been the case earlier. The sectional crisis of the 1850s and the Civil War that followed were a destructive, chastening period for those who thought that national parties could always contain and manage conflict by stressing differences and loyalties that transcended region and section. Some issues had proven to be too big to be effectively handled through partisan means indefinitely.[31]

Nevertheless, parties had significantly delayed the sectional crisis. And when the smoke of war finally cleared in 1865, the basic institutional structure, ideological purposes, and normal operations of American politics had not changed at all. The central reality of a partisanly defined and directed political nation remained dominant. Two national parties, and the competitive party system they comprised, continued to be the core of the political nation after the Civil War, as they had been since the 1830s.

JOEL H. SILBEY

"The Tyranny of Party" Had to Be Broken

Throughout the years of partisan hegemony in America, there were always present on the political scene tensions that reflected the older lines of conflict between individualist antipartyism and those elements successfully pushing to aggregate and discipline the landscape. Those who held to an earlier individualist, purist mentality, which stressed the autonomy of each person to behave in politics unencumbered by other pressures, especially by collectivist disciplining, remained persistently hostile. They strongly resisted the notion that the only possible policy achievements and political successes could come through partisan collective action, action that stressed negotiation, compromise, a willingness to accept delay, half loaves, and incompleteness in achieving one's purpose, as well as a strong tendency to avoid the most contentious issues.[32]

But the tensions present in such formulations remained unfocused and well controlled until, in the aftermath of the Civil War and amid the widely publicized corruption of Reconstruction and post-Reconstruction party activities, antipartyism took firmer hold and grew more vocal and demanding than it had been for a half-century past. In the 1870s and 1880s, a range of Liberal Republicans, Mugwumps, and Independents found their voice and added strength to an intellectual (and often class-rooted and anti-populist) challenge against the notions, ways, and power of political parties in American culture. Their message was clear-cut and simple. "The tyranny of party," they vigorously and relentlessly reiterated, had to be broken.[33]

At first, the dominant partisan vision successfully resisted such challenges, as it had successfully done for half a century past. Parties were never stronger in their reach, authority, and meaning, or in the loyalty exhibited to them, than in the 1870s and 1880s. Civil War memories, if anything, deepened commitment to them and the role that they played. But in the next decade, their power broke and produced the beginnings of one of the most revolutionary transformations American politics has ever undergone, the disruptive dividing moment between two quite different courses of American political development.

Suddenly, something seemed deeply wrong in America, and a sense of fear and impending chaos permeated influential parts of the nation's consciousness. The political and social uproar of the 1890s, an economic dislocation and social shock of unprecedented power, complete with levels of labor and agrarian unrest previously unknown and the frightening Populist and Bryanite challenge to the country's dominant political norms, led to a major electoral destabilization that ultimately went far beyond the usual course of such realignments—to turn into a more fundamental transformation of the American political nation.[34]

Critical analyses of America's threatened condition became a staple of much of the public discourse of the 1890s. At the center of these analyses was the widespread and repetitively circulated notion of the limits and failure of the current political system as it was organized and as it operated. Good-government types had been asserting that partisan politics were corrupt. Parties now also appeared to be ineffectual, had proven easy to take over by dangerous elements, and thus had themselves become a threat to good order, while being clearly inadequate to meet the changing needs of a modernizing nation. American politics, more and more critics forcefully argued, had to be basically reformed.[35]

At the same time and as part of these negative reactions to partisan politics, economic elites—representing the new industrial order coming to dominance and transforming the nation—joined the fray on behalf of a new kind of controlled, predictable politics, a politics responsive to their particular needs. The notion of insulating complicated policy decisions from a too easily aroused and too easily manipulated electorate was never far from the minds of these economic entrepreneurs. As a result, their alternative political economy had little space for parties. Parties were too wedded to their own traditions. They had become barriers to needed changes.

These modernizing elites joined with the good-government reformers to launch a bitter assault on the partisan system. Both saw their campaign as overthrowing a discredited way of politics. Their assault was well financed, well directed, well articulated, and very powerful. In a stunning reversal, equal to what had occurred three-quarters of a century before (albeit in the opposite direction), political parties became the enemies of the people, of good government, and of good purposes.[36]

Such powerful notions found fullest articulation with the new century and the rise of Progressivism as a force on the national scene. The Progressive movement has been the subject of much scholarly scrutiny and constant reinterpretation. Whatever else they were, Progressive reformers were bitterly hostile to political parties, partisan outlooks, and the tradition of aggregative compromise in dealing with political problems. To them, like their Mugwump and Independent predecessors of the 1880s, parties were the great failure of the American experiment. They did not serve democracy's needs. They had become, Progressives claimed, either the servants of the great economic interests dominating the scene or were so preoccupied by their own search for power and plunder that they abjectly failed to fulfill their claimed purposes. Progressives demanded something better than excessive expediency and the sordid manipulation of people and issues. They elaborated, instead, a politics that largely rejected the arts of partisan political management.[37]

The story of what ensued is well known. In the name of reform, Progressives and their allies significantly advanced the attack already under way and succeeded in undermining the existing partisan-dominated political system. As part of their wider program to liberate and modernize American society and control social and economic excess, they mounted a massive rhetorical assault on parties and politicians, seeking to delegitimize both in the eyes of the people. Their assault tellingly redefined politics away from partisan notions, engaging in widespread assaults on the legitimacy of political parties.

An intense debate erupted about the future of the parties, once more framed by their opponents as unresponsive, duplicitous, and corrupt institutions, a framing that emphasized their vulgarity and irrelevance, their quality of being out of touch with the times, their serving as barriers to the activities necessary to deal with a society in need of an untainted, orderly, and systematic political process. What was needed instead, the Progressives and their allies argued, were strong-minded independent people, free from the trammels of party commitment. Only such nonpartisan (really antipartisan) leadership and voters could provide for the needs of twentieth-century America.[38]

The assault accomplished its immediate objectives. Between the 1890s and World War I, a political era emerged in the United States that was ideologically, structurally, and behaviorally different from what had gone before. The dormant, but never absent, antipolitical and antiparty tendency in American culture grew into a popular orthodoxy, at least among many in the nation's expanding, secularized, and educated middle and upper classes. This process of undermining some of the critical elements organizing American politics scored impressive victories. The Progressives and their allies successfully enacted laws that began the process of weakening party control of nominations and voting, as well as providing alternative, nonpartisan channels to force issues onto the political agenda.[39]

No level of government, from Congress to city halls, escaped assault (and reform) in the name of nonpartisanship. And almost immediately, the assault began to open up the political nation to alternative ways—much less coherent ways—of organizing, focusing, and expressing political resources and purposes. Progressives and their allies were delighted. A widening arc of individuals celebrated such independence from parties, their stifling discipline, and their unacceptable behavior. These individuals had little patience for arguments that appreciated the larger societal and political functions that Democrats and Republicans had been performing for so long.

But why did they succeed in carrying out such critical changes as thoroughly as they did? Such powerful transformations as occurred in the Progressive era are never easily accomplished, and one with the enduring impact that this one had is rare indeed, particularly given the earlier history of the excesses of faction in the United States. The extent of the changes seems particularly startling. The answer is not easy to spell out, except to emphasize the accumulation of a series of elements that played on one another to produce a very different political world in the United States. The case against parties was relatively easy to make. Parties had been guilty of many of the charges made against them; they had often been more corrupt than people would accept; they too often delayed or avoided effective challenges to existing iniquities; and they did serve as a barrier to the needs of a new political economy.[40]

All this had something to do with their weakened ability to resist the reformist onslaught. The failures of both the Democrats and Republicans were incessantly noticed and played upon. The charges struck a deeply resonant cord among Americans who had internalized very different political values from their ancestors. And condemnation of evil and corruption, as always, was popular and politically effective at a moment of great societal stress. In a nation increasingly uncomfortable about the widely perceived negative side and failure of parties, the momentum became irresistible. As a result, American political life entered an era that was to be dominated by, in the words of James MacGregor Burns, the "wasting away of parties."[41]

The Real Taproot for Postwar Politics

Such a comment suggests something much more profound than just a range of institutional reforms designed to clean up politics, although that is where it began. As a result of the rhetorical and legislative attacks on the party system, a whole set of changes began to percolate through the political world, from the decline in partisan control of nominations and revisions in voter registration laws, to the reduction in the number of elections held as more offices became appointive, to the loss of a great many of the partisan patronage opportunities that had previously existed, to the decline of close party competition in many areas of the country, a competition that had energized parties and given significant meaning to their activities, to a change in the membership, role, and behavior of policymaking and policy executing institutions.[42]

Each of these activities became less directed by the kind of collective, aggregating political agencies than had previously been the case and was once considered necessary. Progressive reformers and their allies were assailing, and they ultimately significantly crippled, a system of aggregation, linkage, and political socialization—all important elements in allowing our potentially fragmented politics to function at some level of effectiveness. More to the point, these changes, and what they represented, were the initiating point of a long process of extraordinary political modifications that percolated through the system, accompanied by the significant decoupling of Americans from the previously central impulses of their political world—the commitment to the system and the cohesion of the whole—that political parties had brought. Without them, the political landscape became largely devoid of institutions able to anchor and meld the system's many elements, including its voters, in sustained and effective ways.[43]

What happened did not occur all at once or take finished shape immediately. Parties did not immediately wilt. They continued to participate in politics and government throughout the post-Progressive era. Antiparty changes seeped through the system at different rates. But they cumulated in a powerful way across time, ultimately affecting voters, policymakers, political leaders—and everything else as well. Changes in communications, in campaign financing, in the way policy issues were organized and articulated, in the ability of candidates and policy interests to reach beyond party leaders, the decline of those community-based impulses that had done so much to institute and repeatedly reinforce party loyalty and give force to the partisan organization of political life: all took their toll and accumulated, over time, to create a very different political landscape. A new political era had dawned.[44]

Voters reflected much of this shift and the erosion of party authority from the beginning of the transformation, although there was a persistent partisan quality to their actions for a time. In the first decade of the twentieth century, many voters were removed from the rolls by the new "nonpartisan" registration laws in both North and South. At the same time, fewer of those who were eligible to do so bothered to turn out on election day: the proportion of the American electorate that actually came to the polls continued to shrink from its partisan-era character, even when, ultimately, more and more people were admitted to eligibility over the first half of the twentieth century. Very high turnouts had been a hallmark of the partisan political era, often reaching 80 percent of the eligible range coming to the polls on any given day. Sometimes these figures went even higher. In contrast, turnout has not exceeded two-thirds of those eligible since 1900. Not since World War I has even half the electorate cast ballots in off-year elections. Turnout in the nominating primaries has never been high, whatever the Progressive insistence on their democratic character.[45]

Some of this decline resulted from the harshness of the laws passed to manage and "clean up" elections and the impact of racial prejudice in the South. Much of it stemmed, however, from changes occurring in the way that politics was now carried on. Political awareness had not always been automatic or self-generating among Americans. That truth was clearly demonstrated with the decline of parties. The whole widespread, locally rooted network of partisan activists with their range of meetings, rallies, and conventions, sharply declined in numbers and reach. With all of them went the intense, repetitive linking of individuals and their interests to the party system, linkages that had previously made them dedicated, active, and frequently satisfied citizens of the political nation. What voter indifference and volatile behavior revealed was their disconnection from the system and their confusion about what was at stake.[46]

Such shifts in political approaches and behavior were not limited to electioneering and to popular voting behavior. All of the creative political impulses, including policymaking, shifted from the smoke-filled rooms and the hustings to boardrooms, administrative agencies staffed by civil servants, and courts interpreting both the actions of administrative agencies and the various antiparty election laws. In the emerging organizational society of technicians, bureaucrats, and people who thought like them, nonpartisan interest groups began to replace party leaders as the primary shapers of public policy. The changes in voting behavior weakened the parties outside the electoral arena, particularly in their ability to mediate among conflicting groups and make them cohere on behalf of some larger purpose. They no longer had the means to do such. As Daniel T. Rodgers has written, an "explosion of scores of aggressive, politically active pressure groups" filled the space left by "the recession of traditional political loyalties."[47]

These new players had few or no ties to the party system and continued to have no faith in the mass politics the latter practiced. Among all of them, the instinct for working together, except on an ad hoc, often unpredictable basis, weakened. From Congress to state legislatures, the collaborative impulse was less sure. Instead, leaders looked to their own specific interests and individual needs, rather than to a party's position. Of course, such tendencies had always existed. But the balances were clearly shifting to give them a dominance not enjoyed in the partisan era.

Conclusions

At first glance, the New Deal years after 1933 seem to be a major challenge to my argument of cumulative partisan decline. A classic electoral realignment in the 1930s not only returned the Democrats to power with a new policy agenda but also invigorated partisan voter loyalties, fired by the depression and the Roosevelt administration's response. Republican voters, as well as their Democratic enemies, found a new intensity and commitment that seemed as deeply held as anything seen earlier. Party leaders also bounced back in their influence amid this more interested and committed electorate. Policy-making had an intensified partisan edge to it as Democrats and Republicans squared off over the beginnings of the welfare state and more widespread intervention by the federal government into economic life. In such an atmosphere, the reversal of partisan decline and, instead, renewal, reinvigoration, and a persistence of the positions and loyalties established, seemed truly to be the political hallmark of the 1930s.[48]

In truth, the third political era, from the 1890s to the 1940s, was at first glance analytically messy—a mixed bag marked by a mixture of partisan and nonpartisan forms and practices. But I would argue that such partisan renewal as occurred in the 1930s was only a brief wrench in the long-term pattern of partisan decay. While parties existed and their names carried some weight, identified candidates for office, and pressed policy initiatives, they no longer had the force of management and direction they had previously possessed. Despite the New Deal regeneration of partisanship among voters, the continuation of the driving nonpartisan impulses, the disaggregation of politics and the decoupling of individuals from a coherent collective response, continued to penetrate throughout the system.

Policymaking, for example, was more and more disconnected from the hustings except in the most general way. New Deal expansion of governmental authority and the way government operated, primarily reacting to the specific demands of different interest groups, helped this along. Moreover, a strong current existed among New Dealers that contributed to the further weakening of the parties despite their apparent reinvigoration. Franklin Roosevelt, Sidney Milkis argues, believed that the power of the presidency needed to be enhanced even if this meant the further decline "of collective and partisan responsibility." Therefore, Milkis suggests, "the Democratic party became during the late 1930s the party to end all parties," in favor of establishing the presidency "as the principal focus of representative government in the United States." As such, these efforts continued a trend that had existed for a long time. And they continued to have a significant impact on American political life. Certainly, by World War II, the power and reach of nonpartisan interest groups dominated American policymaking. And they worked in such a way as to suggest how little party labels and party visions counted in the rarefied air of an increasingly powerful national government.[49]

Among voters, the New Deal "revival" of parties did not lead to voter turnout at the levels it had manifested in the partisan era a half-century earlier. Similarly, while New Deal-inspired loyalties to one party or the other remained anchored in place for a time after the end of World War II, the subsequent behavior of those who did turn out to vote demonstrated how much the long-range tendencies remained in control. Ultimately, there was to be far more volatility in people's behavior at the ballot box than at any time since the 1820s, first in a dealignment from, and then a nonalignment with, partisan commitments. Parties remained important to some, but were increasingly irrelevant to many. As a result, the connections among elections, policy outcomes, and satisfaction with politics were less and less clear as time passed. Whatever the occasional, even powerful, flare-up in the parties' role and activities, they were not the mainstay of the political nation they once had been.[50]

The important analytic matter remains that while there were different political impulses present throughout the first half of the twentieth century, each with their own distinctive qualities, their cumulative tendencies nevertheless lay in a similar direction and aggregated into something quite different from what had preceded them. Certainly by 1945, at the end of America's third political era, parties were only a pale imitation of what they once had been, their influence occasional and unsustained. They continued to operate and exercised influence in a number of places. But their lack of authority and their limited role grew clearer and clearer. Party decline had advanced far enough to be on the verge of tipping over into a new, less ambiguous situation, one much more fragmented and chaotic than the nation had seen for a century and more.

As a result of all these matters, by the end of America's third political era, the political nation no longer contained a powerful aggregating center able to overcome the fragmenting realities of the constitutional system, of the political economy, and of the political culture. To repeat an earlier point, American politics is crippled without such an aggregating center, given the extent of inherent fragmenting forces. As a result, political leaders found that they no longer commanded a critical weapon for the forging of majorities in the voting and policymaking realms. And voters found themselves cut off from those institutions that had effectively organized and directed their behavior.

The parties had worked very hard to forge and sustain mass allegiances to themselves, and through them, to the system as a whole. Politics counted, they argued, and voters responded to that appeal. Without them and their activities, however, a critical element forging commitment, cohesion, and control was missing—and missed. The institutions that replaced them were not coalition minded in the traditional ways of democratic politics. The American political landscape was littered with fragments of power but lacked effective unifying institutions. Without the road maps parties had provided, without their infrastructure promoting connection and coherence, the American political nation was now the setting of a very different, individualistic, and certainly more volatile political world.

The main point that I am suggesting is, I hope, clear. The elements that define the current political scene in the United States, the nation's fourth distinct political era, one marked by the rapid and seemingly irreversible unraveling of the central institutions of political consciousness, expression, and behavior, have led to our present discontents. They are not a function of the 1960s alone, but of a much longer-range process of change present since the 1890s and of a persistent ideological and behavioral dissonance in American political life. The forces of volatility, disaggregation, nonpartisan cooperation, and increasing reliance on direct action rather than electoral activity were all well advanced long before American troops went into Vietnam in strength, President Lyndon Johnson had lied to the American people, the cities had erupted, and anyone had yet moved into the Watergate complex. They were rooted in our past, in an earlier era's values and attitudes, and in the transformations in our political ways launched at the beginning of the twentieth century. Whatever happened to promote these conditions in the 1960s merely accelerated and confirmed what was already under way.

All of which returns us to the beginning. American politics has remained contentious. In fact, it has grown more and more contentious as a result of the great expansion of organized groups fighting to shape governmental policies in their behalf. In some ways, the American political system has become more open. The access and expectations of many groups to government has significantly increased through their own awareness and organization. But the ability to sort them out and establish priorities has declined. Throughout the massive changes of the past century, not as much attention has been given to managing, integrating, and controlling pluralism as has been directed toward allowing it full rein on the political landscape.

Parties still exist and often can muster a significant polarizing of the political world. In some limited electoral and legislating areas, they retain force. But their reach and range are very limited, particularly in comparison with their former situation. In no way do they shape and direct matters as once they did in any extensive or repetitive ways so as to provide systemwide coherence. Their remains on the political landscape are just that, remains. Without the parties and what they once did for the political nation, we have returned to where we began two centuries ago. We have again empowered chaos, and given new meaning to such terms as fragmentation, factional warfare, and gridlock.[51]

An increasingly demand-driven system has been unable to respond effectively and has provided, in consequence, extraordinarily fertile ground for widespread public frustration and resentment. Fueled by the antics of a hyperventilating press that has increasingly become the main definer and agenda setter in the political nation, in a way that had never previously been allowed for in anyone's philosophy, a disintegrative political model now snugly fits the scene: a highly volatile electorate, a kaleidoscope of pressure points, an increasingly fragmented bureaucracy, all kinds of ad hoc arrangements attempting to manage what appears to be unmanageable, the worst excesses of interest group pressures, presidents under constant siege, a people disconnected from their political world, except through often unfocused and incoherent surge reactions against perceived political inadequacy. But these are matters for my successors in this volume to confront and explore.[52]

Notes

1. *The Guardian,* 28 April 1994.
2. Paul Kennedy, *The Rise and Fall of the Great Powers: Economic Change and Military Conflict from 1500 to 2000* (New York: Random House, 1987). "Ironically, the philosophic ascendancy of liberal democracy is accompanied by growing discontent with its practical operations. From Moscow to East St. Louis, from Mexico City to Cairo, despair about public institutions deepens." Robert Putnam, *Making Democracy Work: Civic Tradition in Modern Italy* (Princeton: Princeton University Press, 1993), 3.
3. Robert Dahl, *The New American (Dis)Order: An Essay* (Berkeley: Institute of Governmental Studies, 1994); and Joel H. Silbey, *The End of American Politics* (Berkeley: Institute of Governmental Studies, 1993), introduce the abundant scholarly literature on this point. See also Walter Dean Burnham's stimulating *The Current Crisis in American Politics* (New York: Oxford University Press, 1982), which originated many of the ideas associated with the theme of American political decline. For a recent popular gloss on our current condition, see Jonathan Rauch, *Demosclerosis: The Silent Killer of American Government* (New York: Random House, 1994).
4. Larry Sabato, *Feeding Frenzy: How Attack Journalism Has Transformed American Politics* (New York: Free Press, 1991); Richard C. Leone, "What's Trust Got to Do with It?" *American Prospect* 17 (Spring 1994): 78–83.
5. Gordon S. Black and Benjamin D. Black, *The Politics of American Discontent: How a New Party Can Make Democracy Work Again* (New York: Wiley, 1994).
6. Walter Dean Burnham, "The Politics of Repudiation—1992: Edging Toward Upheaval," *American Prospect* 3 (Winter 1993): 33.
7. *New York Times,* 24 November 1993, A21; Black and Black, *Politics of American Discontent,* 4.
8. See the essays in Byron E. Shafer, ed., *The End of Realignment? Interpreting American Electoral Eras* (Madison: University of Wisconsin Press, 1993).
9. *The Economist,* 16–22 April 1994, 32; Silbey, *End of American Politics,* 9–10 and footnote 10. Even the usually morose Kevin Phillips, reacting against what he sees as too much emphasis on declinism at the political level, suggests that "democratic renewal—this country's proud speciality over more than two centuries, once again may be in sight." *Time,* 13 June 1994, 53.

10. Joel H. Silbey, "Beyond Realignment and Realignment Theory: American Political Eras, 1789–1989," in Shafer, *End of Realignment?* 3–23.

11. Dahl, *New American Political (Dis)Order,* 1–2.

12. Rauch, *Demosclerosis,* 20. As the *New York Times* put it, "The [Vietnam] war ... planted the seeds of doubt and discouragement about government in the minds of the electorate and the news media." 4 February 1994, A8.

13. Silbey, "Beyond Realignment and Realignment Theory." My primary focus in that article, in my other work cited here, and in this essay is on elements of political management, control, and system maintenance, that is, on how Americans have made their political society cohere and function since the late eighteenth century. Such an approach includes within it many other strands—ideological, cultural, and behavioral—and involves the interactions among elites, the people, government, and interest groups, and in particular the institutional arrangements constructed to carry on American political life.

14. Joel H. Silbey, *The American Political Nation, 1838–1893* (Stanford: Stanford University Press, 1991), 6–10.

15. Richard Hofstadter, *The Idea of a Party System: The Rise of Legitimate Opposition in the United States, 1780–1840* (Berkeley: University of California Press, 1969); Richard P. McCormick, *The Presidential Game: The Origins of American Presidential Politics* (New York: Oxford University Press, 1982); and Silbey, *American Political Nation.*

16. This perspective is central to the analytic work of Walter Dean Burnham, from whom I have drawn insight and inspiration about these matters. See especially his *Current Crisis in American Politics.*

17. William N. Chambers and Walter Dean Burnham, eds., *The American Party Systems: Stages of Political Development* (New York: Oxford University Press, 1975); Paul Kleppner et al., *The Evolution of American Electoral Systems* (Westport, Conn.: Greenwood Press, 1981).

18. Silbey in Shafer, *End of Realignment?*

19. Ibid. See also Silbey, *American Political Nation,* 237 ff.

20. The limitations of the Constitution as an effective governing instrument have been a major theme in the work of James MacGregor Burns. See, for example, *The Deadlock of Democracy: Four-Party Politics in America* (Englewood Cliffs: Prentice Hall, 1963), and his many other works.

21. Silbey, "Beyond Realignment," 7; Ronald P. Formisano, "Deferential-Participant Politics: The Early Republic's Political Culture, 1789–1840," *American Political Science Review* 68 (June 1974): 473–87. J. Roger Sharp refers to the Federalists and Republicans of the 1790s as "proto-parties," *American Politics in the Early Republic: The New Nation in Crisis* (New Haven: Yale University Press, 1993), 8.

22. Lacey K. Ford, "Inventing the Concurrent Majority: Madison, Calhoun, and the Problem of Majoritarianism in American Political Thought," *Journal of Southern History* 60 (February 1994): 22; Robert E. Shalhope, *The Roots of Democracy: American Thought and Culture, 1760–1800* (Boston:

Twayne, 1990).

23. Henry Jones Ford, *The Rise and Growth of American Politics: A Sketch of Constitutional Development* (New York: Macmillan, 1898), 93.

24. Hofstadter, *Idea of a Party System;* McCormick, *Presidential Game;* Chambers and Burnham, *American Party Systems;* and Silbey, *American Political Nation.*

25. U.S. Congress, *Register of Debates,* 19th Cong., 1st sess., 1546.

26. Silbey, *American Political Nation,* chaps. 1–2.

27. Ibid., passim.

28. *Congressional Globe,* 26th Cong., 1st sess., appendix, 52; 30th Cong., 1st sess., appendix, 775.

29. Silbey, *American Political Nation,* chaps. 4–10.

30. Michael F. Holt, *The Political Crisis of the 1850s* (New York: Wiley, 1978), covers these matters in excellent style.

31. Ibid.; William E. Gienapp, *The Origins of the Republican Party, 1852–1856* (New York: Oxford University Press, 1987).

32. Richard L. McCormick, *The Party Period and Public Policy: From the Age of Jackson to the Progressive Era* (New York: Oxford University Press, 1986), 228–59.

33. *Report of the National Executive Committee of Republicans and Independents, Presidential Campaign of 1884* (New York: 1885), 23.

34. Burnham, *Current Crisis in American Politics;* Samuel T. McSeveney, *The Politics of Depression: Voting Behavior in the Northeast, 1893–1896* (New York: Oxford University Press, 1974).

35. Richard L. McCormick, *From Realignment to Reform: Political Change in New York State, 1893–1910* (Ithaca: Cornell University Press, 1981); Kleppner, *Evolution of American Electoral Systems.*

36. Samuel P. Hays, *The Response to Industrialism, 1885–1914* (Chicago: University of Chicago Press, 1957); Robert Wiebe, *The Search for Order, 1877–1920* (New York: Hill and Wang, 1967); and McCormick, *From Realignment to Reform.*

37. Ibid.

38. In addition to notes 36 and 37, see Arthur S. Link and Richard L. McCormick, *Progressivism* (Arlington Heights, Ill.: Harlan Davidson, 1983).

39. Hays, *Response to Industrialism;* and Wiebe, *Search for Order,* cover this ground.

40. McCormick, *From Realignment to Reform.*

41. James MacGregor Burns, *The Power to Lead: The Crisis of the American Presidency* (New York: Simon and Schuster, 1984), 140.

42. Lewis Gould, *Reform and Regulation: American Politics from Roosevelt to Wilson,* 2d ed. (New York: Knopf, 1986). The electoral consequences of this reformist onslaught are discussed in Paul Kleppner, *Continuity and Change in Electoral Politics, 1893–1928* (Westport, Conn.: Greenwood Press, 1986).

43. Silbey, *American Political Nation,* 237–54.

44. Michael McGerr, *The Decline of Popular Politics: The American North, 1865–1928* (New York: Oxford University Press, 1986).

45. Walter Dean Burnham, "The Turnout Problem," in *Elections, American Style,* ed. A. James Reichley (Washington, D.C.: Brookings Institution, 1987), 97–123; William Gienapp, "Politics Seems to Enter into Everything," in *Essays on American Antebellum Politics, 1840–1860,* ed. Stephen Maizlish and John Kushma (College Station: Texas A&M University Press, 1982), 18–23; and Paul Kleppner, *Who Voted: The Dynamics of Electoral Turnout, 1870–1980* (New York: Praeger, 1982).

46. McGerr, *Decline of Popular Politics.*

47. Daniel T. Rodgers, "In Search of Progressivism," *Reviews in American History* 10 (December 1982): 4.

48. Kristi Andersen, *The Creation of a Democratic Majority, 1928 to 1936* (Chicago: University of Chicago Press, 1979); John Allswang, *The New Deal and American Politics: A Study in Political Change* (New York: Wiley, 1978).

49. Sidney Milkis, *The President and the Parties: The Transformation of the American Party System since the New Deal* (New York: Oxford University Press, 1993), 5.

50. Martin Wattenberg, *The Decline of American Political Parties, 1952–1984* (Cambridge: Harvard University Press, 1986).

51. Theodore J. Lowi, *The End of Liberalism: Ideology, Policy, and the Crisis of Public Authority* (New York: Norton, 1969).

52. Dahl, *New American Political (Dis)Order.*

SOCIETY

Michael Barone

Our Country:
The Shaping of America
from Roosevelt to Clinton

T HIS CHAPTER BEGAN as a lecture on American politics at Nuffield College, Oxford, to an audience whose acquaintance with the subject was certainly greater than that of Nuffield's founding Warden, Sir Harold Butler. Sir Harold described himself as being, at the time of the 1919 peace conference, "totally ignorant of American politics and American ways of thought." "None of us," he wrote of his circle, "realized what a different type of western civilization had grown up in the United States in the nineteenth century, how under American conditions a different social philosophy and a different political system had evolved."[1] Today, partly because of work done at Nuffield, that obviously is no longer so. And yet we must hurry to keep in place, for the American civilization and politics that grew up in the nineteenth century have been replaced, gradually and with occasional juddering, by a civilization and politics that have now had practically all of the twentieth century to evolve.

The "Old Country"

Think of how different from the America of today was the America that Franklin Roosevelt steered through the Great Depression and led into war. That America had only half as many people and an economy only one-fifth the size of the America of today.[2] Even more important, the mind of the country was different. At the center of American politics was still the conflict between North and South. "The impact of the Civil War on American life and American memory can hardly be exaggerated," wrote one British student of America. "It is still 'the war.' "[3] Amazingly, this was written in 1944, in the midst of a struggle that, for Americans my age and older, was for so many years "the war," though few Americans think of it that way anymore, only fifty years after D-Day. In 1929 and 1930, southern Democrats in Congress protested that they would be oppressed by the Smoot-Hawley tariff as they had been by the War between the States, while northern Republicans proclaimed that they had won then and would win this time too. Note that on even this apparently economic issue, the real fervor came from the cultural split between the regions. Another measure of the chasm of this regional split is that between 1865 and 1940 something on the order of 5 million Americans migrated from North to South, despite the vastly higher wage rates in the North, while 35 million immigrants crossed the Atlantic during the same years.[4] That United States was, in Robert Wiebe's phrase, a "segmented society,"[5] divided far more profoundly along lines of region, race, religion, and ethnic origin than by economic status.

The America of half a century ago had a vital politics built around two political parties, both already old, both capable at their best of adapting to the multivarious and always changing country they sought to govern. There is an enduring asymmetry to the two parties: Thomas Nast was right to portray them as two different animals. The Democrats, the oldest political party in the world—with an unbroken series of quadrennial national conventions since the one assembled by Martin Van Buren to nominate Andrew Jackson for a second term in 1832—have always been the party of out-people, of those who feel and are felt by others to be somehow not entirely American, and who at their strongest have become the in-party of the nation. The Democrats have been the party of southern slaveholders and segregationists and Irish Catholic immigrants, unionized factory workers and prairie-parched farmers, smug Washington insiders and angry blacks and feminists.[6] At their worst, they have been a ragtag assemblage, a party that "ain't on speakin' terms with itself," as Finley Peter Dunne's Mr. Dooley put it in 1900 (and could have said in the 1860s, 1890s, 1920s, and 1970s). At their best, they have been the in-party of a vibrant and expansionist nation, in times as widely separated as the 1840s, 1910s, 1940s, and 1960s.

The Republicans, the third-oldest party in the world,[7] have always been the party of a central faith, to which they cling with an almost religious tenacity, confident that this faith represents what Robert Kelley calls the American "core culture"[8] and unembarrassed by its almost total lack of support from some large segments of the electorate.[9] The original Republican faith was that of small-town Protestant Yankee reformers, the intellectual offspring of Ralph Waldo Emerson and Harriet Beecher Stowe. They believed in free labor and free soil, and they made a civil war that ended slavery. They then enacted an energetic program of high tariffs, free homesteads, land-grant colleges, and a transcontinental railroad. With rare intellect and rhetorical skill, Theodore Roosevelt updated this Republican faith and directed its reformist impulse to the outer world.[10] This impulse animated the mostly unelected Republicans of the foreign policy establishment through the early 1960s, even as the faith of elective Republicans at home soured as their small-town strongholds were beset by the New Deal.

This was the country and these were the political parties called on to respond to the unexpected economic collapse of the 1930s. It has come to be conventional wisdom that Americans responded with demands for economic redistribution. But in 1932, after economic product had declined by 50 percent in four years, the Communist Party candidate for president got 102,000 votes, the Socialist candidate got 884,000, and the candidate of the Democratic Party, for years the party of low tariffs, low taxes, and governmental decentralization, got 22.8 million. The central feature of Franklin Roosevelt's first New Deal of 1933 and 1934 was not change but stasis, a series of wage and price controls intended to stop the downward economic spiral. Impractical as long-term policy, these short-term expedients were followed by some economic growth, the spiral was broken, and the Democrats were rewarded by the voters, winning House seats in the off-year elections of 1934, the only time this has happened in the twentieth century.

It also produced a major partisan realignment.[11] Before the 1930s, the politics of voters of immigrant stock was entirely local: in New York, they voted Democratic; in Philadelphia, Republican; in Chicago, they were up for grabs. Beginning in 1934, they voted heavily Democratic almost everywhere. Democrats made vast inroads in the coal and steel heartland of West Virginia, Pennsylvania, and Ohio: another permanent change. The parts of the country that had been classic swing areas in the old political order—the Progressive Upper Midwest and West Coast, the Jewish ghettos of New York and other big cities—now voted heavily Democratic.

Importantly, this change occurred before the second New Deal, the economic redistributionist programs endorsed by Roosevelt in May and June of 1935—the Wagner labor act, Social Security, steeply progressive tax rates. The 1936 Roosevelt landslide was a carbon copy of the 1934 results: a verdict more on the economic upturn of 1934 and early 1935 than on the class-warfare rhetoric of 1936. The second New Deal did create new American institutions, those industrial labor unions spawned by the United Mine Workers' John L. Lewis, the United Steelworkers, and the United Auto Workers. But voters responded negatively to redistributionist efforts after 1936: the sitdown strikes of 1937, the minimum wage of 1938, the third New Deal executive reorganization bills of 1938 and 1939. New Deal Democrats lost control of Congress in 1938 and failed to regain it in the next four elections. Roosevelt himself, polls make pretty clear, would have lost in 1940 and 1944—in all likelihood he would not have run—if those elections had been decided on domestic issues and not the war.

Then came the war. Far more than the depression or the New Deal, World War II changed America, shaped it into a different sort of country, a country whose culture and politics stayed much the same for a long generation. The war was a nationalizing experience, a time in which the whole nation was mobilized and in which almost everyone underwent similar experiences. In 1940, 48 million Americans were working in jobs or in the military; in 1944, 65.5 million were[12] —an amazing increase in just a few years. In 1940, the federal government was spending $9.6 billion; in 1944, $94 billion.[13]

This was a war that was won by—and to a large extent created by —the big units of American life: big government, big business, big labor. On the surface, electoral politics seemed to become a struggle between big business and big labor for influence with big government, but in fact the stakes were always marginal. Neither the Wagner Act nor Roosevelt's wartime labor regulations created the syndicalist state that business leaders feared. Just as the Taft-Hartley Act, passed after the Republicans' landslide victory in the 1946 off-year elections, did not destroy the labor movement. It confined it to the ground it held: textiles would never be unionized, autos always would be.

The governmental programs that would incline most voters after the war to favor the Democrats on economic issues were not 1930s New Deal redistributionist programs that helped the poor but 1940s policies that encouraged, rewarded, subsidized, and honored those who were working to move themselves up the ladder: the GI Bill of Rights with its generous payments for college educations, the FHA and VA home mortgage guarantees that helped transform a nation of renters into a nation of homeowners, and the family allowance created by the combination of the steeply graduated income tax and generous deductions for dependents, which helped subsidize the baby-boom generation. The America of the long generation after 1940 was a country whose people worked contentedly and productively as parts of big units, a country criticized for its conformity and groupmindedness, but a country of both individual initiative and communal responsibility, of economic growth and creativity, of educational excellence and low crime and violence.

The Postwar World

In this America, despite the surface hubbub over economic issues, cultural issues more often proved decisive, as they usually have in American history. In 1948 the Democrats won a victory, their biggest in the twenty years following 1936, and along straight-ticket lines.[14] But in 1949 they failed to pass their bills for civil rights (opposed by southerners) and federal aid to education (opposed by Catholics, who wanted their parochial schools aided too). They were put on the defensive by foreign developments: the fall of China to communists in October 1949 and the North Korean attack in June 1950 on South Korea, to which the United States responded in the name of the United Nations. While most Republicans supported the NATO alliance in 1949 and the stationing of U.S. troops in Europe after 1950, many Republicans and some Democrats criticized the administration for "losing China" and, after the firing of General Douglas MacArthur in April 1951, for not seeking victory in Korea. Some focused on the presence of communists, of whom a few actually were in government before the mid-1940s. But the biggest hubbub came after 1950, when communists were long since removed but when clever politicians such as Richard Nixon tried to use this cultural issue to split the majority party and charlatans such as Joseph McCarthy used it to aggrandize himself, until his predictable ruin.

The wonder of the 1952 election was not that the Republicans won after twenty years out of power but that they won by such a modest margin as 55 to 44 percent, especially when the prestige and experience of their candidate, Dwight Eisenhower, far exceeded that of the nonetheless attractive Democrat, Adlai Stevenson, and when the Democrats refused even to promise an end to the Korean War that was killing 25,000 Americans a year. This is evidence that, foreign policy issues aside, the Democratic New Deal majority was at its demographic peak, a few years after the big cities' percentage of the population peaked and just a few years before the unionized percentage of the workforce reached its high, in the election year when turnout zoomed from 48 million to 62 million as the GI generation fully entered the electorate. Dwight Eisenhower, like Bill Clinton a long generation later, came to power as a candidate of the minority presidential party. But, unlike Clinton, Eisenhower had the assets of military renown, moral authority, and a steely self-discipline to shun policies he personally favored but thought politically unpopular (like cutting tax rates and domestic spending). The commander of the largest amphibious invasion in history proved a congenial leader of a country where people were happy to work and live in big units.

This country began the next decade with confidence in its leaders and basic institutions and ended it in disillusion and distrust. The 1960s are a fulcrum point in American history: the glamour of the Kennedy administration and the horror of the Kennedy assassinations, the glorious success of the civil rights revolution and the mindless violence of riots in every major city, the success of American technology in the space program and the debacle of American management techniques in Robert McNamara's prosecution of the war in Vietnam. It was also the first full decade in which Americans had grown used to seeing their presidents and politicians on television. The media of political communication have changed several times in the twentieth century and give signs of changing again today. In 1900 the premium was on rhetorical eloquence. William Jennings Bryan could hold an audience of 30,000 people for three hours without amplification; Theodore Roosevelt's vibrant words on the printed page provided new visions of the Republican Party's place in America and America's place in the world; Woodrow Wilson revived the practice of delivering his State of the Union message in person to Congress and inaugurated the practice of the president's traveling abroad to meet foreign leaders at the summit and accept the cheers of foreign crowds in the streets. Rhetoric communicated political ideas at a high intellectual level, while cultural allegiances, transmitted through party newspapers and other media targeted at specific segments, channeled the vast numbers of votes of ordinary people.

Then, suddenly, radio became a universal medium: 5 percent of households had radios in 1924, 27 percent in 1928, 61 percent in 1932—an amazing gain after four years of depression—70 percent in 1936, 80 percent by 1940.[15] Franklin Roosevelt was aware of this trend. He crafted his 1924 speech nominating Al Smith for the audience in the hall, but in 1928 he wrote a calmer, more chatty speech intended for the radio audience. By March of 1933, he was delivering his trademark fireside chats over the radio, speaking simply and succinctly to the ordinary people he envisioned gathered around the radio set, explaining the complexities of the world in clear and reassuring language.

After Roosevelt's death, television became a universal medium even more rapidly than radio had: less than 1 percent of households had television sets in 1948, 34 percent in 1952, 71 percent in 1956, 87 percent in 1960.[16] Television made Estes Kefauver a presidential candidate when he investigated organized crime in 1951; it unmasked Joe McCarthy for the bully he was in 1954; it showcased the reassuring face of Dwight Eisenhower, who used media advisers, and did less for Adlai Stevenson, who spurned them. Television was the medium over which Americans became used to the crisp, self-assured articulateness of the young John F. Kennedy; famously, voters who listened to the first presidential debate of the 1960 campaign on radio thought that

MICHAEL BARONE

Richard Nixon won, but most of those who watched on television—a much larger number—said Kennedy did.[17]

But it was only in the 1960s, especially in the event-filled year of 1963, that television developed the technology that brought footage of even violent news events instantly into Americans' family rooms and kitchens and started broadcasting the thirty-minute evening newscasts that for two decades became the town squares of American politics. In May 1963, Americans saw Bull Connor's police dogs and fire hoses attack Martin Luther King's peaceful demonstrators in Birmingham; in June 1963, they saw Ngo Dinh Diem's troops attack Buddhist monks in Hué; in August 1963, they saw 200,000 civil rights marchers gathered before the Lincoln Memorial in Washington; in November 1963, they saw the murders of John Kennedy and of his assassin, and watched his funeral.[18] Television brought tragedy into every household and exposed mercilessly the defects of the American system and American leaders, which other media allowed citizens to gloss over.

And there were more defects than had been apparent on the surface. Americans started the 1960s nervous about events but confident of the soundness of government and other basic institutions. But the big units that had structured American life since World War II—big government, big business, big labor—were becoming corrupted, and the newest generation of Americans, the postwar baby boomers, found them confining and hateful. Remember that the first student riots of the 1960s came before the escalation of the Vietnam war, in Berkeley in September 1964. The university's president, Clark Kerr, had proclaimed the era of the "multiversity," another big unit; one of the demonstrators' cries was, "Do not bend, fold, or mutilate"—do not treat me as an IBM card, as one fungible component that is part of an enormous mass.

The corruption of big business was exemplified by the Big Three auto companies, whose supposed managerial brilliance was shown by the appointment of the woefully unprepared and unwise Robert McNamara as secretary of defense in 1961. By the mid-1960s, the Big Three were producing defect-loaded cars with "planned obsolescence," confident that their near-monopoly would enable them to pass along generous wage and benefits increases to consumers who could be persuaded to buy any product by advertising. This was, after all, the way things worked, as explained by John Kenneth Galbraith in *The New Industrial State*,[19] a book published just as rising import sales were showing that this was not the way things need always work: that big units could suffer terrible penalties for poor performance. Big labor was corrupt as well; even Walter Reuther's United Auto Workers, with its social-democratic vision, acquiesced in shoddy production and urged its members to "take it easy, but take it." Labor leaders enjoyed the good life, even as they watched their membership rolls slowly shrink.

The corruption of big government was shown most vividly in the big unit that had won total victory in World War II, the American military and its civilian leadership. The strategists of the Kennedy and Johnson administrations made a war in Vietnam that they did not ask their own sons to fight. The decision to take responsibility for the governance of South Vietnam, a decision taken in August 1963 when John Kennedy on a summer weekend approved the coup to overthrow Ngo Dinh Diem, came just as the first baby boomers were about to turn eighteen and register for the draft. A cynic would say that America sent half a million men to Vietnam just as its manpower pool vastly increased. Policymakers retained the World War II draft, with plenty of exemptions—for college and graduate students, for those with flat feet or psychoneurosis or orthodonture. The draft threatened college students and became unpopular on campus, yet the student exemptions meant that most college-educated males never served.

Instead, they not only protested the war but heaped discredit on the government and the country they refused to serve. This was not the only force producing what social scientists called "alienation" among the young college-educated and the wider population as well. The success of the civil rights movement in changing the nation's mind and discrediting one major institution—legalized racial segregation as it had existed in the South—cast doubt on the legitimacy of every institution. The Kennedy assassination, coming not at a moment of triumph as had Abraham Lincoln's assassination and Franklin Roosevelt's death, violated the comforting symmetry of American history and contributed to a sense of randomness and disorder. Crime rates, low by any historic standard since the 1930s, suddenly began to rise; campus rebellions and urban riots followed in 1964, 1965, 1966, 1967, and 1968. Government was failing to meet its first duty, providing an order in which people could go about their daily lives, and confidence in government began falling rapidly.

And government success in managing the macroeconomy was followed by failure. The sustained low-inflation economic growth of the 1960s was replaced by unexpected "stagflation"—stagnation and inflation—in the 1970s, and as government grew larger and took on more tasks, confidence in its efficacy declined. Just as the depression of the 1930s and the war effort of the 1940s convinced most Americans that markets did not work and that government did, so the stagflation of the 1970s and the growth of the 1980s would convince most Americans that government does not work and markets do. If the breadlines of the 1930s helped create a Democratic majority, so the gasoline lines of the 1970s pushed toward a Republican majority.

The Return of Cultural Politics

In this suddenly disordered America of the late 1960s, there was, not surprisingly, another political realignment. Southern whites—Democratic as late as 1956 and 1960—turned against both the Kennedy-Johnson administration and the national Democrats once Kennedy came out for the Civil Rights Act in June 1963. They would accommodate themselves more readily to integration of public accommodations and workplaces than anyone expected, but their disagreement with the foreign policy dovishness and cultural liberalism of the national Democrats would keep them voting Republican, even when born-again Christian southerner Jimmy Carter was nominated in 1976. Blacks—oscillating between the parties in 1956 and 1960—began in 1964 to vote overwhelmingly Democratic. Central-city margins for Democrats fell after 1960 and 1964; they had been inflated because John Kennedy had received 78 percent of Catholic votes in 1960, when his Catholicism was an issue for many Americans (63 percent of white Protestants voted for Richard Nixon that year). But you can elect a first Catholic president only once, and afterward, Catholic Democratic percentages regressed toward the mean, while Catholics and other whites were leaving the increasingly dangerous cities for the suburbs.

The cultural divide in American politics was no longer between Catholic and Protestant, North and South, city and countryside. It was a divide along lines of values, in which those who believed in liberation from the traditional mores of 1940s America were on one side and those who believed in honoring those values were on the other. This transformation was apparent by the 1968 election and was exacerbated by the fact that the elites of America, especially in the political and communication capitals of Washington and New York, were moving rapidly toward the liberation side, while most voters, especially in the South and in the growing suburban rings around the shrinking central cities, were rallying to the traditional standard.

This basic division in American politics continued for most of three decades, quite as long as the regional and ethnic divisions, with their spotty overlay of economic differences, that prevailed from the mid-1930s to the mid-1960s. The parties were still asymmetric. The Democratic Party remained a collection of out-people, at times just enough of them to be the in-party at the White House. It was strong in Congress and legislatures because it remained flexible enough to attract talented politicians capable of adapting to local circumstances and attracting support from national lobbies that, until the Republican landslide of 1994, maintained its majorities in the House and, with the exception of six years in the 1980s, in the Senate. In presidential elections, Democrats have become weakest now in their historically strongest area, the South; their new heartland has become the northern tier of the country, from New England and New York, across the Upper Midwest, and including varying amounts—quite a lot right now—of the West Coast.

This has been the party's core when it has nominated northern tier candidates—Hubert Humphrey, George McGovern, Walter Mondale, Michael Dukakis—and remained strong for Democrats even when they nominated southerners Jimmy Carter and Bill Clinton. Here cultural liberalism is strong. This is the most dovish, even isolationist, part of the country, where American intervention is seen as dangerous to them and evil to us; it is most supportive of liberation from traditional sexual mores and gender roles, a set of attitudes for which support of legalized abortion has become the proxy; it is the place where the caregiving professions, teachers and social workers especially, became organized by public employee unions and imbued with the liberal values of their leaders. Since the 1970s, the focus of liberal Democrats has shifted from foreign policy dovishness to racial representativeness to what is now the primary source of élan and enthusiasm in the Democratic Party, feminism.

At the 1992 convention, four of the five labor unions most heavily represented at the Democratic National Convention were public employee unions, with heavily female membership. Bill Clinton's 1992 campaign is famous for consultant James Carville's slogan, "It's the economy, stupid!" and in fact owes much of its victory to George Bush's conspicuous uninterest in domestic issues. But the VRS exit poll shows that the sharpest divisions among American voters were not along economic lines but according to religion—and not by historic denomination but by degree of faith. It also shows that in most large states, voters with graduate-school degrees voted more Democratic than those who graduated from college only: these are the teachers and social workers and lawyers who give Democrats their base in middle- and upper-income precincts.

The Republicans—demoralized in the 1970s by the ouster of Richard Nixon, inspired in the 1980s by the success of Ronald Reagan, puzzled in the 1990s by the inattention of George Bush—have remained the party of a central faith. But the nature of that central faith has changed. In the early 1970s, it was the faith of an older generation, people who had come of age in the 1920s and before, baffled by student protests and urban riots, people who had conceded grudgingly the unwisdom of America's Vietnam strategy and the unfairness of racial segregation but believed in the fundamental principles of a system that the protesters insisted was rotten. By the late 1970s, as the American economy was threatened with hyperinflation and America was in humiliating retreat abroad, the GI generation, the people who had come of age in the years of Franklin D. Roosevelt, yearned for the control over events domestic and foreign that Roosevelt had exerted; and they elected an old New Deal Democrat, Ronald Reagan, who in two elections carried 93 of a possible 100 states.

Reagan's success in office was unparalleled since Roosevelt's. His policies produced seven years of low-inflation economic growth at a time when Democrats said that was no longer possible, along with a victory in the Cold War that was foreseen by only two active American politicians, Reagan and Daniel Patrick Moynihan. (Is it significant that both are of Irish descent?) Far more than Richard Nixon, who in office expanded domestic government and pursued détente with China and the Soviet Union, Reagan strengthened belief in America's special mission in the world and its special goodness as a nation.

The strongest believers in this new central faith, and the new demographic core in the Republican Party, is the religious right, believers in traditional religious and moral values who feel under siege from a hostile media and from hostile caregiving professions who run public-sector institutions in line with their own values rather than those of the public. Economic issues in America today are less an argument over the distribution of income—any conceivable economic policy changes that distribution very little—than they are an argument between those who want more money to go to a public sector imbued with liberation-minded values and those who want the money to remain with a private sector where tradition-minded values are free to compete in the marketplace of ideas. It is a choice, if you will, between therapy and discipline, a choice that parties offer on issues from crime to foreign policy to public employee strikes—and even in their candidates' personalities.

The America of today is a more segmented society than the America of the post–World War II era, a country in which economic growth and the bulk of jobs come from small units rather than big units, a country in which most of us live in our own subdivisions and condominium developments, attend our own churches or encounter groups, watch our own cable channels, without much regard for neighbors who a mile or even a block away might be living in a very different America. Universal institutions that brought almost everyone together, like the comprehensive high school and the universal military draft, have disappeared. Voters no longer throng to the electronic town square of American politics, as network news viewership is down and voters seek their information from congenial sources, from National Public Radio to Rush Limbaugh and other talk radio programs.

Big-city neighborhoods and rural small towns are no longer so cohesive; the distribution of income, steady between 1947 and 1973, has been growing less egalitarian ever since. For those who see post–World War II America as the norm, the quintessence of the national experience, all this is disturbing. It is less troubling if the big-unit America, the one that grew up suddenly during World War II and persisted for a long generation after, is seen as the exception and not the rule in American history. The segmented, high-tech, hip-hop America of today to me resembles in many important ways the America of the years before 1940 or 1914, in its small-unit economy, its cultural variety and even cultural hostilities, its ambivalence about engagement with the world beyond.

There are differences, of course. Americans at the beginning of this century were embarked on what Robert Wiebe called a "search for order,"[20] using bureaucracy and government to discipline huge agglomerations of wealth and power. Americans today are engaged in a search for autonomy and empowerment, trying to live and work and engage in Tocquevillian community life outside and beyond the big units that have become corrupt and unresponsive and in some cases have withered away and died. American political analysts are finally getting over looking for a return of the New Deal Democratic coalition and pondering whether there is an emerging Republican majority. Now we need to get used to a cultural politics revolving around personal values, a politics centered on things as important to today's Americans as the Civil War and racial/religious/ethnic differences were to Americans in times past.

What next? People's politics do not change in time with regular cycles, but in response to the events that cut to the quick of their lives. Americans were shaken and moved by the disorder of the early 1930s and the disorder of the late 1960s; nothing has so shaken us since, and we must hope that nothing will again soon. So in the spirit of Sir Harold Butler, let us try to realize what a different type of Western civilization has grown up in the United States in the twentieth century and to understand today's America and its politics, so different from what Americans my age grew up with, so eerily reminiscent of the America of a century and more ago.

Notes

1. Harold Butler, *Confident Morning* (London: Faber and Faber, 1950), 162–63.

2. Michael Barone and Grant Ujifusa, *The Almanac of American Politics 1990* (Washington, D.C.: National Journal, 1989), xxiv.

3. D.W. Brogan, *The American Character* (New York: Knopf, 1944), 44.

4. Michael Barone, *Our Country: The Shaping of America from Roosevelt to Reagan* (New York: Free Press, 1990), 17–18. On the South as a "low-wage region in a high-wage country," see Gavin Wright, *Old South, New South: Revolutions in the Southern Economy since the Civil War* (New York: Basic Books, 1986), 71–78. In 1920, fewer than 2 million native Americans born in the South lived outside the region. *Historical Statistics of the United States* (Washington, D.C.: U.S. Department of Commerce, 1975), 89–93.

5. Robert H. Wiebe, *The Segmented Society: An Introduction to the Meaning of America* (New York: Oxford University Press, 1975).

6. Michael Barone, "Can They Save the Party? Bill Clinton and Al Gore May Bring New Life to the World's Oldest Political Party. Or They Could Preside Over the Democrats' Last Hurrah," *U.S. News & World Report*, 20 July 1992, 24–28.

7. If one counts Britain's Conservative Party as beginning in the 1840s and concedes a tie with Canada's Progressive Conservatives, who also trace their start to 1854.

8. Robert Kelley, *The Transatlantic Persuasion: The Liberal-Democratic Mind in the Age of Gladstone* (New York: Knopf, 1969).

9. Michael Barone, "The Woes of Living with GOP Ghosts. Bush, Unlike Lincoln, Teddy Roosevelt, and Reagan, Hasn't Created a Unifying Faith," *U.S. News & World Report*, 24 August 1992, 34, 39–41.

10. See Stephen Skowronek, *The Politics Presidents Make: Leadership from John Adams to George Bush* (Cambridge: Harvard University Press, 1993).

11. Michael Barone, *Our Country*, 74–75.

12. Ibid., 154.

13. Ibid., 165.

14. Despite the fact that there were third- and fourth-party candidates—just as the 1992 elections saw more party-line voting than in any intervening contest, despite the candidacy of Ross Perot. See Michael Barone and Grant Ujifusa, *The Almanac of American Politics 1994* (Washington, D.C.: National Journal, 1993), xxvii–xx.

15. *Historical Statistics of the United States,* 796, 42.

16. Ibid.

17. Barone, *Our Country,* 331–32.

18. Ibid. 352–56, 386–88.

19. John Kenneth Galbraith, *The New Industrial State* (Boston: Houghton Mifflin, 1967).

20. Robert Wiebe, *The Search for Order, 1877–1920* (New York: Hill and Wang, 1967).

INSTITUTIONS

CHARLES O. JONES

Separating to Govern:
The American Way

I N HIS REFLECTIONS entitled *Two-Hundred Million Americans in Search of a Government,* the straight-talking political scientist E.E. Schattschneider observed that "Democracy is a political system for those people who are not too sure that they are right."[1] As it happened, Schattschneider spent much of his professional career urging American political parties to state what was right and proposing reforms to enable them to be effective. But I like his depiction of American democracy for a reason that would displease him. I consider it a clear statement of the rationale for a separated system of governing, one characterized by the competing legitimacies that logically interfere with the capacity of political parties to do what Schattschneider and others judged to be right.

The American system of separated institutions does not show well. It invites criticism and reform, both of which are functional for its operation. There is, in fact, continual tension between what many analysts want to see in governing and what they are likely to get with separationism. Most perspectives on the American national government are based on the classic responsible-party, presidency-centered model. In this perspective, political parties should be prepared to overcome constitutional separation, primarily through presidential leadership. What many such analysts have in mind, of course, is the clarity and elegance of the British political system. If the United States could just form a government, responsibility would surely follow. When the government acted correctly, it would be rewarded; when it did wrong, it would be punished. Lloyd Cutler, a man with substantial experience as a counselor to presidents, is an articulate advocate of this viewpoint:

> In parliamentary terms, one might say that under the U.S. Constitution it is not now feasible to "form a Government." The separation of powers between the legislative and executive branches, whatever its merits in 1793, has become a structure that almost guarantees stalemate today....
>
> Although the enactment of legislation takes only a simple majority of both Houses, that majority is very difficult to achieve. Any part of the president's legislative program may be defeated, or amended into an entirely different measure, so that the legislative record of any presidency may bear little resemblance to the overall program the president wanted to carry out.
>
> ... because we do not form a Government, we have no overall program at all. We cannot fairly hold the President accountable for the success or failure of his overall program, because he lacks the constitutional power to put that program into effect.[2]

Inconvenient factual errors undercut this analysis. First and foremost, it simply is not correct that stalemate is guaranteed within the separated system. A president may, indeed, find that his proposals are not ratified in form and in turn by the House and Senate. But lawmaking does proceed. Whether or not a government is formed in Cutler's terms, landmark legislation is enacted. What of the New Deal? the Great Society? the Great Tax Cut of 1981? Those are outstanding cases of a president having his way, no doubt pleasing the advocates of party government if not dedicated separationists.

Split Partisan Control

The great worry for these advocates, however, remains the penchant of American voters for returning split-party government—a president of one party with the other party having majorities in one or both houses of Congress. A system of disconnected or independent elections, deemed essential for the purity of the separation of powers, does lack a structural feature for ensuring partisan unity.

As it happened historically, the frequency of split-party results during the latter half of the nineteenth century (occurring 45 percent of the time, 1856–1900) abated substantially during the first half of the twentieth (occurring just 13 percent of the time, 1900–1946). That development, along with conditions facilitating the strong presidencies of Woodrow Wilson and Franklin D. Roosevelt, unquestionably encouraged the champions of party government. At long last, the American system was maturing. We would have government!

Imagine the discontent among these advocates when split-party government reemerged as a common pattern during the latter half of the twentieth century. However difficult it is to form a government (in Cutler's terms) when one party wins all three elected branches, it is well-nigh impossible with the two parties sharing power in the separated system. Stalemate is said to be the result.

Scholars of comparative political systems agree with the advocates of party government regarding the probability of stalemate in what they label "presidentialism." Thus, for example, Arend Lijphart cites deadlock as a disadvantage to presidential government. "The problem of executive-legislative conflict, which may turn into 'deadlock' and 'paralysis,' is the inevitable result of the co-existence of two independent organs that presidential government creates and that may be in disagreement. When disagreement between them occurs, there is no institutional method of resolving it."[3]

CHARLES O. JONES

The stalemate or gridlock scenario is logical enough, I suppose, for those believing that it is necessary to "form a government" in the parliamentary way. After all, how is there to be lawmaking if the prime minister and cabinet are of one party and the House of Commons or the Diet or the Storting another? It does not necessarily follow as an outcome within a separated system, however. After all, what is the measure of stalemate? Surely it is not just the failure of the president to have his way. No one can believe that a system of independently derived and constitutionally mixed institutions would automatically and consistently accede one to the other.

What, then, is the test of stalemate or gridlock? The production of major legislation is a defensible indicator. If no laws are passed, there is gridlock; if laws are passed, the system is not gridlocked. David R. Mayhew of Yale University has examined exactly that issue in his book *Divided We Govern*. He first created an elaborate two-wave process for identifying major legislation, then simply took a look. He found that major legislation is enacted by both single- and split-party governments.

In fact, there are no significant differences in the post–World War II period—an average of 12.8 major acts passed during single-party Congresses, an average of 11.7 major acts passed during split-party Congresses.[4] It is of particular note that three Congresses tie for the highest production of major legislation (at twenty-two each): the 89th (Johnson's first full Congress), the 91st (Nixon's first), and the 93d (Nixon's third—completed by Ford). Most analysts would have predicted that the 89th Congress would be included; few would have identified the Nixon Congresses as being in that group.

It is true, of course, that different political combinations will produce different *solutions* to the same public problems. There are differences in the policy goals and representation of interests between the two political parties. But having variable policy outcomes dependent on the configurations of political control is not stalemate—at least by the ordinary understanding of the term.

There is more that is questionable about the party-government perspective. The much-admired parliamentary systems do not all provide responsibility as advertised. I make mention of the Japanese system since it has been so prominent in the news in recent years. What exactly is the public accountability of a multiparty coalition government? Are not the compromises that are displayed publicly in a separated system often developed in less public settings in a coalitional government? How are the voters to determine responsibility in a government that includes socialists and conservatives? Who exactly is accountable for what? One report on 1995 local electoral defeats for the ruling coalition noted that

> The results raise new doubts about whether [Prime Minister] Murayama and his governing coalition, a marriage of convenience between Socialists and conservatives, can stay in office for the rest of the year. The 70-year old prime minister has been savaged recently for inaction on major national problems, and members of his own coalition seem to be moving away from him.[5]

Lloyd Cutler yearns for a president to form a government "with a legislative majority which takes the responsibility for governing." But it seems that there is no magical formula for that happening in any system. Or that, having taken action, a government will necessarily invite being held responsible. Forming majority coalitions in the American political system is extremely demanding. The effort to do so is unceasing, since one coalition does not necessarily hold for the next issue. What is required, therefore, are "the skills of political management," not the transformation of the system.[6] I turn next to a review of the post–World War II experience to illustrate the range of skills required for governing, with special emphasis on the challenge of leadership facing the president.

Separated Institutions Competing for Shares of Power

The results of disconnected elections are difficult to read, even if they are endlessly fascinating to me and my colleagues. Voters are given various forms of expression to vent even contradictory moods and opinions. The vote in a parliamentary or strong-presidential system is quite efficient, but it carries a heavy weight. Once delivered, it triggers a process of government building, at least for the political side of government. But in a separated and federalized system, voters can roam freely across independently chosen bodies, putting a Democrat here, a Republican there—having it both ways through the layers of government, which are themselves interdependent. We do not really have elections in the parliamentary sense. We have political *fairs,* in which many contestants go home winners. And voters like it that way if we are to believe the polls, not to mention the frequency of their ticket splitting.

Attention here is directed to the national level. It is worth recalling, however, that a program proposed by a Democratic president, and altered by a cross-party coalition in Congress in which the Republicans serve as a majority, may then be administered by a Republican governor and legislature, to deal with problems in a city with a Democratic mayor and council. Political parties are organizations of convenience for facilitating policy action in the separated system. They are not free-standing entities.

Consider the ballot itself and the scheduling of elections (as associated with term lengths). The ballot provides the choices. Its exact form is determined by the states, where various arrangements have been tried over the decades either to encourage or discourage party voting. Scheduling was once the province of the states, but the many inconveniences caused by differing election times led Congress to set a uniform date, the first Tuesday after the first Monday in November. Even with that change, however, variable term-limits preserved and enhanced separationism.

A freshly elected president may be encouraged by congressional election results that produce a majority of his party in the House of Representatives and the Senate. He may even have the short-term advantage of a perception among these new members that he had something to do with their election or reelection, though such views are not common. Yet House members are no sooner elected than they must begin to think about reelection, which, if they have a challenger in the primary election, may be only eighteen to twenty months away. Moreover, at the point of their reelection, the president will not be on the ballot; in fact, there is no national election as such at the midterm, just national results.

Presidents vary in their willingness to participate in these midterm elections, since active involvement may invite the interpretation of having been defeated. Besides, the record of the president's party at midterm is not encouraging: an average loss of thirty seats during the post–World War II period, with a range of four to fifty-five seats. On just three occasions did the number fall below ten—for Kennedy in 1962, Reagan in 1986 (his second term), and Bush in 1990 (when Republicans had just 175 seats to start).

Scheduling for Senate elections is substantially more perverse from the president's perspective. Imagine that a president won overwhelmingly and that his party gained seats in the Senate, thus inviting the identification of a coattail effect (e.g., 1980). First, just one-third of the senators are up for reelection at the point of his triumph (a group that was itself elected six years earlier and may represent a skewed party split).[7] Second, those elected may indeed be grateful if they believe the president had a positive influence on their win. But their reelection bid comes in six years, at the midterm of the president's second administration (if there is to be a second administration). On what basis does the president have an electoral hold on those few senators who might have thought he was an asset for their election? They will never again see him on their ballot.

The next one-third will be elected at the midterm of the president's first administration and will be up for reelection at the point at which the president's stay in office will have ended (with the two-term limitation). The final one-third will be elected on the president's reelection and may also profit in the best of all possible political worlds from the president's coattails. But their term carries forward to the midterm of the next president. And the last senatorial election in a two-term presidency produces a class that is up for reelection with the new president six years hence (see figure 3.1).

There is more. As noted, voters have ample opportunities to split their vote, and they do. The result has been frequent split-party governments in the post–World War II era, as voters have become comfortable electing Republican presidents and Democratic Houses, Senates, or both. Of all electoral college votes cast in presidential elections from 1948 to 1992, 63 percent were awarded to Republican presidential candidates (who won seven of twelve elections, six by electoral college landslides). Yet Democrats held majorities in the House of Representatives for a record forty years, 1954–94, and in the Senate for a period of twenty-six years, 1954–80. Prior to 1994, Republicans held House majorities just three times and Senate majorities six times in the postwar period.

Three newly elected Republican presidents (Nixon, Reagan, and Bush) and three reelected Republican presidents (Eisenhower, Nixon, and Reagan) faced Democratic majorities in one or both houses. One Republican (Eisenhower) and one Democrat (Clinton) watched their parties' majorities disappear at midterm. And one takeover president for each party (Truman and Ford) faced opposition majorities in Congress.

The point is clear enough. Elections do not automatically produce unity, even when one party wins both branches, and certainly not when the parties share control of three elected branches—the presidency, the House of Representatives, and the Senate. Building supportive coalitions is continuous, involving as it does a constant effort to

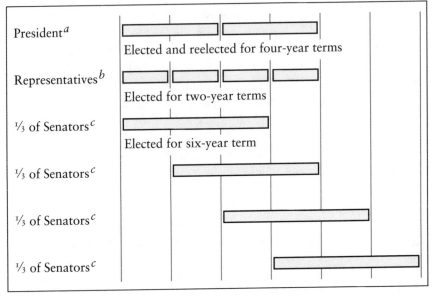

FIGURE 3.1
ELECTORAL TIME LINE: PRESIDENT (TWO-TERM),
REPRESENTATIVES, AND SENATORS

a. Since 1951 and the ratification of the Twenty-Second Amendment, presidents are limited to two terms. In this century, only six presidents have been elected to second terms (FDR to four); only four completed their two terms (FDR completed three).

b. The president's party typically loses seats in the midterm election (with just one exception in this century—1934). Major losses were experienced in 1910 (57), 1914 (59), 1922 (75), 1938 (71), 1946 (55), 1958 (47), 1966 (47), 1974 (43), 1994 (52).

c. Note that no group of senators elected during these eight years again runs with the president on the ballot!

convince representatives and senators that what the president wants is in their own best interests, or vice versa. All of that is demanding work on the part of political and legislative strategists, since very few members of either chamber will view their political and electoral fates as closely connected with that of the president.

It seems apparent, therefore, that a strictly partisan strategy for building coalitions is often inapt. Instead, presidents and congressional party leaders must devise cross-party strategies for two quite different legislative bodies—the House and Senate. Reforms that seek to strengthen party discipline and unity falter in the face of an electoral and representational system that fosters copartisan, cross-partisan, and bipartisan lawmaking. I understand that it is difficult for the "form a government!" advocates to accept, but the American political system relegates political party to a facilitating, not an assertive or controlling, role.

Many Presidencies

There is an understandable practice of marking historical periods by presidents, for example, the Roosevelt, Eisenhower, or Reagan era. And though we may label presidents as strong or weak, we seldom do more than identify the whole period of service as their presidency. I do acknowledge that dividing history by the presidents who serve is a convenience. But it also follows in the separated system that any one period of presidential service may be characterized by change. There may, in fact, be *more than one presidency per president,* if defined in terms of the political and policy advantages available to the incumbent in working with Congress.

I have classified each president in the past hundred years by his political advantages upon entering office, at midterm, and, for six presidents, on reelection (see table 3.1). After that, I first examined four-year terms of service, noting the stability and change of advantages following the presidential and midterm elections (see table 3.2). The range is from huge advantages (a landslide presidential election combined with substantial congressional majorities) to weak minority status (a president facing formidable opposition-party majorities in Congress). The results of this analysis show the following:

1. Relatively few presidents sustain substantial advantages over a four-year period. In fact, there are only three clear cases: Franklin Roosevelt's first and second terms, and the one full term of Theodore Roosevelt.
2. Four presidents had relatively stable advantages over four years —two with moderate political status, two with weak status (their party being in a minority in Congress).
3. Two administrations maintained moderate advantages through four years, but the presidents changed (McKinley to Roosevelt; Kennedy to Johnson).
4. Most common are modest or substantial changes in advantages as a result of midterm elections. Sixteen of the presidencies fall into this classification, with eight demonstrating modest but notable shifts and eight demonstrating substantial shifts from one Congress to the next.

TABLE 3.1

PRESIDENTS' POLITICAL ADVANTAGES, 1896–1996, AT PRESIDENTIAL AND MIDTERM ELECTIONS

President	EV	PV	House 1	House 2	Senate 1	Senate 2	President's overall political advantages[a]	
							1st Cong.	2d Cong.
McK1	Mod	Small	Mod	Small	Small	Mod	Mod	Mod
McK2→TR	Mod	Small	Mod	Small	Large	Large	Mod+	Mod
TR	Large	Large	Large	Mod	Huge	Huge	Large+	Large
WHT	Mod	Small	Mod	Min	Large	Small	Mod	Small–
WW1	Huge	Min[b]	Huge	Small	Small	Mod	Large	Mod
WW2	Small	Min	Min[c]	Min	Mod	Min	Small	Min
WGH→CC	Large	Huge	Huge	Small	Small	Mod	Large	Mod
CC	Large	Mod	Mod	Small	Mod	Small	Mod	Small
HH	Huge	Large	Large	Min[d]	Mod	Small	Large	Small
FDR1	Huge	Large	Huge	Huge	Large	Huge	Huge	Huge
FDR2	Huge	Huge	Huge	Large	Huge	Huge	Huge	Huge
FDR3	Huge	Mod	Large	Small	Huge	Mod	Large	Mod
FDR4→HST	Huge	Mod	Mod	Min	Mod	Min	Mod	Min
HST	Small	Small[e]	Large	Small	Mod	Small	Mod	Small
DDE1	Huge	Mod	Small	Min	Small	Min	Mod–	Min+

	EV	PV	House 1	House 2	Senate 1	Senate 2
DDE2	Huge	Large	Min	Min–	Min	Min–	Min+
JFK→LBJ	Small	Min	Large	Mod	Large	Mod	Mod
LBJ	Huge	Huge	Huge	Mod	Huge	Large	Huge	Large
RMN1	Small	Min^f	Min	Min	Min	Min	Min
RMN2→GRF	Huge	Huge	Min	Min–	Min	Min–	Min+
JEC	Small	Small	Huge	Large	Large	Mod	Mod
RWR1	Huge	Small^g	Min	Min–	Small	Small	Mod–
RWR2	Huge	Huge	Min	Min	Small	Min	Min
GHWB	Large	Mod	Min	Min–	Min	Min	Min
WJC	Mod	Min^b	Mod	Min	Mod	Min	Min

KEY TO COLUMN HEADS AND SCALE RANGES

EV = Electoral college vote: 50–59 percent = Small; 60–69 percent = Moderate (Mod); 70–79 percent = Large, 80 percent and above = Huge.

PV = Popular vote: Less than 50 percent = Minority (Min); 50–52 percent = Small; 53–55 percent = Moderate (Mod); 56–58 percent = Large; 59 percent and above = Huge.

House 1 = 1st Congress of an administration; House 2 = 2d Congress of an administration.

Senate 1 = 1st Congress of an administration; Senate 2 = 2d Congress of an administration.

House and Senate ranges are defined by percentages of seats held by president's party: Less than 50 percent = Minority (Min); 50–54 percent = Small; 55–59 percent = Moderate (Mod); 60–64 percent = Large; 65 percent and above = Huge. A plus or minus symbol indicates the top or bottom region of the range it follows.

a. Takes into account both electoral advantages and the margin of seats held by the president's party in Congress.

b. There was a third candidate, Theodore Roosevelt.

c. The Democrats failed to elect a majority in 1916, but Progressives voted with the Democrats to organize the House.

d. The Republicans elected a majority in 1930, but several died before the opening of Congress, enabling the Democrats to organize.

e. There was a third-party candidate, Strom Thurmond.

f. There was a third-party candidate, George Wallace.

g. There was an independent candidate, John Anderson.

h. There was an independent candidate, H. Ross Perot.

TABLE 3.2

STABILITY AND CHANGE IN THE POLITICAL ADVANTAGE
OF PRESIDENCIES, 1896–1996

Advantages	Presidents in category	Number of presidencies[a]
Stable—Substantial advantages		
Huge→Huge	FDR1, FDR2	1
Large plus→Large	TR	1
Stable—Moderate advantages		
Moderate→Moderate	McK1, JEC	2
Stable—Few advantages		
Minority→Minority	RMN1, GHWB	2
Stable advantage, change in presidents		
Moderate plus→Moderate	McK2→TR	2
Moderate→Moderate	JFK→LBJ	2
Changing—Modest shift (variable advantages)		
Huge→Large	LBJ	2
Large→Moderate	WW1, WGH→CC, FDR3	7
Moderate→Moderate minus	RWR1	2
Moderate→Small	CC, HST	4
Small→Minority	WW2	2
Changing—Substantial shift (variable advantages)		
Large→Small minus	HH	2
Moderate→Small minus	WHT	2
Moderate→Minority	FDR4→HST, RWR2, WJC	7
Moderate minus→Minority	DDE1	2
Minority plus→Minority minus	DDE2, RMN2→GRF	5
Total		45

SOURCE: Compiled by the author, based on data in table 3.1.

a. A presidency for these purposes is defined as one in which there has been a change in advantage or in president.

What of the reelected presidents? Do any maintain stable advantages through two terms (eight years)? There are but six reelected presidents in this century, four of whom completed two terms (Roosevelt completed three). McKinley and Franklin Roosevelt had the most stable presidencies for two full terms—McKinley with moderate advantages throughout (though succeeded by Theodore Roosevelt in 1901), Franklin Roosevelt with huge advantages in his first two terms. Franklin Roosevelt's second two terms were less impressive, eventually resulting in an opposition-party Congress after Harry Truman became president. The three reelected Republicans in the post–World War II years, Eisenhower, Nixon (succeeded by Ford), and Reagan, demonstrate somewhat similar patterns—mostly a stable set of limited advantages until the second midterm election, when the Democrats strengthened their hold on Congress. Finally, Woodrow Wilson's presidencies display a steady decline in advantages from large to moderate to small to minority status (see table 3.3).

TABLE 3.3

STABILITY AND CHANGE IN POLITICAL ADVANTAGE
FOR REELECTED PRESIDENTS, 1896–1996
(RANKED FROM MOST STABLE TO LEAST)

President	*Stability and change*
McKinley[a]	Moderate→Moderate→Moderate plus→Moderate
F.D. Roosevelt[b]	Huge→Huge→Huge→Huge→
	Large→Moderate→Moderate→Minority
Eisenhower	Moderate minus→Minority plus→Minority plus→
	Minority minus
Reagan	Moderate→Moderate minus→Moderate→Minority
Nixon[c]	Minority→Minority→Minority plus→Minority minus
Wilson	Large→Moderate→Small→Minority

SOURCE: Compiled by author, based on data in table 3.1.

  a. Succeeded by Theodore Roosevelt in 1901.
  b. Succeeded by Harry Truman in 1945.
  c. Succeeded by Gerald Ford in 1974.

In summary, a system of separated elections produces an ever-shifting coalitional base. The numbers change for presidents and Congresses every two years. If we count presidencies as suggested earlier—that is, those cases where there are marked differences in advantages and/or a change in presidents—then I count forty-five presidencies for the eighteen presidents who have served during these hundred years, 1896–1996. One can understand in such circumstances why the "form a government" advocates are distressed. Short of major constitutional restructuring, however, individual presidents, congressional party leaders, committee chairs, and other decision makers need to accommodate the realities of the separated system if we are to make law.

Stability in Congress

Frequent elections and variable terms do not necessarily equate with instability in Congress. Instead, these characteristics pose a challenge for the president for the reasons stated earlier, that is, member allegiance to separate constituencies. The president might conceivably gain an edge, however, if there were high turnover, amateurism, and short memories. No such luck. The House and Senate have come to be increasingly professional, career oriented, and institutionalized. They are repositories of policy knowledge and experience. They have developed a well-articulated committee structure that serves as home base to private and governmental clienteles. And they have created an elaborate staff apparatus that more than matches that immediately available to the White House, albeit not as hierarchically organized.

Consider these facts. Incumbent return remains high in the House of Representatives, typically over 90 percent. By design, Senate incumbent return is 67 percent, to which is added whatever number is reelected (typically somewhat lower than for the House). The average length of service of members during the post–World War II period has typically been about ten years each for the House and Senate. The average for presidents in that same time is half that number.

The president might realize a leadership advantage if congressional leaders changed with each change in presidents. Again, no such luck. The House and Senate act independently in choosing leaders; any change with presidents is purely coincidental. In recent decades, only the Carter administration could take advantage of new party leadership in both the House and Senate coincident with the president's taking office. Alas, as a professed and dedicated outsider, President Carter was not even in a position to view the change as an asset.

Typically, party and committee leaders serve in accordance with the internal politics and traditions of each body. The average service of the two principal House party leaders for 1945–85 was 9.1 years;[8] of the Senate leaders, 6.3 years. Major committee chairs also have had lengthy service, in some cases carrying through several presidents: Carl Hayden, fourteen years as chair of the Senate Appropriations Committee; Russell Long, sixteen years as chair of the Senate Finance Committee; George Mahon, fifteen years as chair of House Appropriations; Wilbur Mills, seventeen years as chair of House Ways and Means.[9]

Professional staff has expanded significantly in the past two decades. Each member has been given additional staff, many of whom are then dispatched to the state or district to aid in perfecting a representational style that will be approved at election time. Committee staffs have become not-so-small bureaucracies, some of which operate outside the orbit of daily congressional politics. New support agencies have been created—the Congressional Budget Office and the Office of Technology Assessment; others, like the Congressional Research Service, have been greatly expanded.[10]

The House and Senate are separate lawmaking enterprises fully prepared by reason of institutional and membership continuity and of professional capability to participate widely in national policymaking. An unusually vigorous term-limitation movement has recently emerged to challenge the whole concept of a career-oriented legislature. The group has had a significant impact: Several members have limited themselves, and freshman classes have demanded more participation, unwilling to accede to the seniority principle that advises them to wait their turn. Term-limit proposals actually reached the House floor for debate during the 1995 hundred-day legislative blitz, though none received the necessary two-thirds majority. Yet, perhaps most important, the term of service of committee chairs was limited to six years by a change in the rules of the House of Representatives.

Are these changes, including term limits, likely to encourage the formation of a "government?" There is no reason to believe that they will. These are not changes designed to alter the separation of institutions or reduce the competition for shared powers. The term-limited Republican freshmen of the 104th Congress appear to be as devoted to controlling affairs in competition with the president as were the Democratic chairmen of the 100th Congress (Reagan's last)—perhaps more so.

Policy Eras

All too often, political scientists discuss institutions devoid of their vital role in the lawmaking and policymaking processes.[11] Yet the separated system exists to act authoritatively on public problems. And so presidents, representatives, and senators, along with their respective staffs, spend much of the working day on substantive issues—many of which are a consequence of laws they passed earlier. Further, these issues are central to how the institutions are organized and how the work gets scheduled. Substantive policy issues permeate a capital, in the physical presence of buildings with names like Department of Agriculture and legislative rooms designated as Committee on Armed Services, as well as in the talk that mostly centers on what to do about what has been done in the past.

Presidents and Congresses work within an agenda orientation that is naturally associated with broad policy developments. Until 1981, we observed a familiar cycle of expansion and consolidation. Government expanded to meet new needs, followed by periods of consolidation wherein the principal effort was to make government more effective in administering new programs (often through reorganization and regulation). The periods of expansion were during the Wilson, Franklin Roosevelt, and Johnson presidencies, each of which was succeeded by consolidation.

In 1980, a president—Ronald Reagan—was elected who judged that government was the problem, not the solution. He questioned whether it was appropriate to make government work better, if to work at all was inimical to the public interest. So for the first time, there was a serious effort to install a contractive agenda. Two approaches were tried. The first was programmatic: seeking to cut back, eliminate, or devolve various federal programs. The second was fiscal: seeking to reduce taxes, thereby starving the revenue side so as to prevent enactment of new programs and to force serious evaluation of existing programs.

The first, program cutbacks, was only marginally successful, given strong opposition from clienteles. The result was great pressure for another kind of solution, that is, increasing taxes again so as to avoid escalating debt and to provide more latitude in policymaking. Taxes were raised several times during the Reagan presidency, but it fell to George Bush publicly to rescind his "no new taxes" pledge. And still the deficits rose, greatly complicating incremental adjustments in existing programs.

During the Reagan and Bush presidencies, it became apparent that serious contraction of government programs simply was not possible.[12] Cutting back lacked political support, and therefore the agenda was dominated by fiscal issues—mostly finding new revenues so as to reduce the deficit. And then along came Newt Gingrich and the "Contract with America." The Democrats were correct in associating the contract with Reaganism. It is the unfinished business of the contractive agenda, that is, serious reduction of government spending as a means for reducing the deficit.

As a result, the version of the separated system following the 1994 elections had these features: a policy-ambitious Democratic president with weak status, a highly energized Republican House of Representatives, a competitive Republican Senate with several presidential candidates, all tackling an intricate contractive agenda. My final thoughts are about these intriguing and historic circumstances, starting with President Clinton's first two years.

President Clinton and the Separated System

Bill Clinton fits with the weakest of the presidents in this century in terms of his political capital on entering office. He won with a minority of the popular vote, 43 percent, and a moderate electoral vote count. There are no coattails, perceived or real, for 43 percent presidents. In fact, Democrats suffered a net loss of House seats in 1992 and failed to gain the hoped-for sixty-seat majority in the Senate, so as to be able to break filibusters.

Why Clinton won at all is relevant to his policy status once in office. Clinton emphasized change in the people who would serve, in the style of leadership, and in the policies enacted. But it is far from certain that his election carried with it an open-ended mandate for dramatic change. The "form a government" analysts were predictably pleased with the results, since the Democrats won all three elected branches. Here is how one such advocate viewed the results:

> If the government cannot succeed in the present configuration, when can it possibly ever succeed? ... the stars are really aligned right for the next four years.
>
> The country has finally gotten back to unified government. For the first time in twelve years, somebody is going to be responsible.... Now the day of buck passing and blame shifting is over.[13]

Another interpretation, one derived from a separationist perspective, might have gone something like this. Many Reagan voters in 1984 and Bush voters in 1988 were displeased with President Bush's performance. The change they desired was for him to leave the White House. Had they had a chance to vote for Ronald Reagan again, they probably would have done so. Even then, a substantial number of this group voted for Ross Perot, not Bill Clinton.[14] There was no mandate for new social programs, including a national health-care plan.

Bill Clinton was instead authorized by reason of his election to use the presidency to persuade Congress and the public of the correctness of his policy views. But there was no escaping the Reagan legacy of debt or the unfinished contractive agenda, for which there was continuing public support. And the charge to the president in a separated system is to fit himself into the permanent government so as to be a credible participant, perhaps a leader. As noted earlier, very few presidents enter with huge advantages, and few maintain those advantages through their term. By this reading, President Clinton needed to compensate for his weaknesses to take full advantage of his constitutional status in the separated system.

What are those weaknesses? Presumably, they are not in campaigning, where he excelled.[15] Instead, he had limitations related to the fact that he was a governor from a small state located at a distance from Washington. He had never held a position in the federal government. While governor, he had worked with a Democratic legislature, seldom ever having to take Republicans into account. Like most governors, he lacked experience with foreign and national security matters. He was an admitted "policy wonk," who found it difficult to concentrate on a few issues. Wishing to please, he frequently engaged in hyperbole, promising more than could conceivably be delivered. Also, the governorship of Arkansas is not a huge management job. Thus Bill Clinton lacked direct experience in forming (and accommodating) to an elaborately articulated staff. "He wouldn't know good staff work if he saw it," was how one member of the Clinton administration expressed it.[16]

What did the new president then do by way of compensating? He relied on his presumed strength—campaigning—instead of overcoming his weaknesses. He did not form an effective staff. He did not work with Republicans, who would be needed for support of his proposals, particularly in the Senate. He postponed foreign and national security issues so as to emphasize domestic concerns (with the exception of early announcements on Haiti, later altered, and the promise of an executive order ending the ban on gays in the military, not fulfilled). He issued a laundry list of proposals, promising early action on very complicated pieces of legislation, most notably health-care and welfare reform.

How effective has his campaigning style been? First, some facts. In his first twenty months in office, he traveled to 150 places, making 203 official appearances, exclusive of travel to Camp David, to Arkansas, to foreign countries, and to vacation sites.[17] He is our most traveled president, exceeding even George Bush, who loved to fly in Air Force One. And Clinton's travel was associated primarily with the selling of public policy proposals. Approximately one-quarter of the travel of Bush and Reagan was for party and candidate fund-raising events. As Clinton's political adviser, Mandy Grunwald, reportedly explained it: "It's a bank shot, what you say to the American people bounces back to the Congress."[18]

Unfortunately, there is limited evidence that this "going public" strategy worked very well in the first two years. One measure might be the public approval ratings. Did they rise with the president's domestic travel? They did not. His quarterly approval ratings in the Gallup poll exceeded 50 percent just twice in the first twenty months in office. And the rating was lowest in the seventh and last quarter for that period. Another measure would be a favorable response among the public to his policy priorities, most notably health-care reform. Again the evidence shows the reverse to be the case; support for his plan declined steadily following his presentation in a special message to Congress in the fall of 1993.

A more substantive measure of presidential success is the passage of major legislation. Three kinds of legislation were enacted in his first year: (1) those bills already in the legislative pipeline, having been vetoed by President Bush (e.g., family leave, motor voter, a waiting period for handgun purchase); (2) the "big ticket" items—the economic plan and NAFTA; and (3) special Clinton initiatives such as lifting the ban on homosexuals in the military, the National Service Act (or "Americorps"), and the "reinventing government" proposals. These accomplishments are significant by Mayhew's count of major legislation[19]—nearly equal to Carter's first year, less than Kennedy's, less than half of what passed in Johnson's first year as an elected president, but markedly more than most Republican presidents with the exception of Nixon.

Can they be said to have been enacted because of the "bank shot"? That would be a difficult argument. The first group passed quickly because they were essentially congressional Democratic initiatives. The second group did not go so well: the economic stimulus plan was defeated in the Senate, the budget reconciliation package passed by a tie-breaking vote from the vice-president in the Senate and by a two-vote margin in the House, and NAFTA was a Bush administration carryover enacted with Republican support. The third set was more purely the president's, but, in fact, was not frequently discussed in his many travels (National Service being mentioned most often).[20] Whatever the explanation, President Clinton could be justifiably pleased with the legislative product in his first year, particularly given his weak political status. And he was rewarded by judgments that he "and the 103d Congress broke through the legislative gridlock that has gripped Washington in recent decades...."[21]

There would be no such plaudits at the end of the second year. The campaign approach to governing continued, with the president taking to the road to sell his program. But there were few positive parallel developments that could contribute to producing a strong legislative record. Major proposals came to produce the congressional equivalent of a logjam at the end of the session, thus granting the Republicans the advantage allowed by the filibuster, at no political cost to them. Among the casualties was Clinton's' health-care proposal, his principal priority. But the list was long of those measures postponed or killed.

The count of major legislation enacted at the end of the session was small; by Mayhew's count, the fewest major bills passed for any elected president in his second year during the postwar period.[22] And the judgments by analysts were harsh: "This will go into the record books as perhaps the worst Congress—least effective, most destructive, nastiest—in 50 years."[23]

President Clinton and the New Congress

The 1994 congressional midterm elections were historic in many respects. No elected first-term Democratic president in this century had experienced loss of both houses of Congress. The win for the House Republicans produced their first majority in forty years, a record length of time in the minority. And having a serious party platform such as the "Contract with America" is unprecedented for midterm elections.

Thus, one can sympathize with the president's political and policy predicament. There were no obvious analogies. The opposition Republicans were extraordinarily energized to assume leadership. Media analysts interpreted the results as constituting a mandate for the House Republicans and a major defeat for the president. And White House political strategists seemingly had failed to prepare a worst-case scenario, leaving a garrulous president virtually speechless.

The consequence was the most unusual, even peculiar, first three months of a congressional session in history. It is unusual for the House of Representatives to set the agenda. It is unusual for either house to produce legislation during the first three months. It is unusual to maintain strong party discipline in Congress. It is unusual for party leaders to manage the House of Representatives in competition with committee chairs. It is unusual for junior members to be a driving force on legislation. Yet all of these things happened. Here are some of the measures of the activity in the House of Representatives during the hundred days:[24]

Hours in sessions:	531
Measures passed:	124
Recorded votes:	302

By comparison, the busier-than-usual first three months of the 103d Congress had been markedly less active by these measures. The 80th Congress, which is sometimes used for comparison, was somnolent (two roll-call votes in the House, seven in the Senate; no completed legislation). Republican Party unity in the House was likewise phenomenal in these first hundred days. *Congressional Quarterly* identified thirty-three votes incorporating the "Contract with America." House Republicans averaged 98 percent unity on these votes.[25] Republicans had perfect unity on sixteen of the thirty-three votes and attracted a majority of Democrats on sixteen of the thirty-three.

Here then was a most interesting case of a presidential-congressional partnership in the first year, disintegrating due to minority-party obstruction in the second year, and then being transformed into congressional domination as a result of surprising election results and the rarity of a midterm party platform, inviting a concocted identification of a mandate for the new Speaker of the House. During the election, one of the president's closest political advisers, Paul Begala, reportedly had revealed that "there is not a night I don't thank God for the contract [with America]."[26] No doubt by April the Contract had come to be a nightly event somewhat more disturbing of sleep for Begala and his client.

I begin my book on the presidency with these sentences: "The president is not the presidency. The presidency is not the government."[27] It is equally true that the Speaker is not the House of Representatives, and the House of Representatives is not the government. Gingrich's hundred days differ significantly from Roosevelt's, in that the Democrats won the presidency, House, and Senate in 1932, at the point of the greatest domestic crisis in the twentieth century. Franklin Roosevelt had authority virtually to act as he thought best. By contrast, and substantially as a result of his own political ingenuity, Newt Gingrich had an opening to move his program through one chamber of a bicameral Congress.

Senate Republicans had not committed themselves to the Contract and, in any event, are part of an institution designed to be more deliberative. They were led by Bob Dole (R–Kans.), a person with ten years' experience as a floor leader (two in the majority) and a leading candidate for the Republican presidential nomination in 1996. He could be expected to act cautiously for institutional and political reasons. Therefore, the Senate would not be expected to act quickly, though it was fully engaged too on the early work necessary to cope with a broad range of Republican initiatives.

What, then, of the president's position under conditions of congressional preponderance? A president with limited domestic policy goals, such as George Bush, or one whose goals have been achieved, such as Ronald Reagan, may adapt rather well to those circumstances. Content to concentrate on foreign and national security issues, such presidents employ the veto to curb congressional excesses and participate in domestic initiatives where political gain is to be realized.

In the case of Bill Clinton, however, this formula was more problematic. First, he is a restless, policy-ambitious chief executive, not one comfortable in responding to the initiatives of others. He is also personally ambitious: he wants to be a great president. But relying on the veto is reactive, not active. Further, the Republicans appropriated many of his issues—tax cuts, welfare reform, line-item veto, governmental reform, relief for the states, even health-care reform—in essence forcing him to redefine his goals within the context of their legislation. Then, as it happens, his anxiety during the first two years to avoid gridlock resulted in his not having vetoed any bills—a modern record. Therefore he had to create a credible veto threat as a means of regaining influence in lawmaking.

President Clinton's virtual exclusion from action on Capitol Hill through much of 1995 provided time for him and his staff to devise a strategy for regaining political status. As revealed in a series of speeches during the first months of 1995, the strategy contained the following tenets:

1. Associate the president with the change seemingly demanded by the voters. Argue that the 1994 results represent a continuation of the mandate for change designated as a consequence of the 1992 election.
2. Remind the public that the president was there first with many of the issues of the "Contract with America"—tax cuts, welfare reform, relief for the states, reducing the deficit—and thus he can be cooperative where possible.

3. Reveal that the president's proposals are more humane, that they represent improving government, not destroying it. Thus he will identify the limits of devolution to the states, measuring proposals by their adverse effects on various clienteles.
4. Search for high profile issues subject to executive order, where congressional action is not required.
5. Threaten the veto primarily as a means for identifying the president's position. Avoid being too specific prior to more explicit Senate action for strategic reasons.
6. State a "no politics as usual" position—getting it right is more important than being reelected.
7. Take full advantage of the uniquely presidential status in foreign and national security issues, as well as national disasters or crises.

Later dubbed "triangulation," the strategy was designed to position the president as the moderate, one who accepted many of the goals of the "Contract with America" (which had, after all, been market tested), but served to protect the beneficiaries of programs whose growth was to be slowed.

The strategy was skillfully executed. Particularly striking was the exercise of the veto. President Clinton rejected major appropriations bills, the debt limit extension, and a massive budget reconciliation package. One risky consequence was the shutting down of the government. As it happened, congressional Republicans were judged by most Americans to be responsible for this unpopular action. Their leaders were no match for Clinton's campaigning style with the public. The president was still not a major player in formulating policy—the agenda continued to be set on Capitol Hill—but he had reestablished himself as a force to be reckoned with.

One final point in regard to the president's status. There have been but three presidents reelected in the postwar period—all Republicans (Eisenhower, Nixon, and Reagan), all three reelected by landslides, all three returned with Democratic congressional majorities in one house or two. Successful cross-party coalition building can be rewarded at the polls. The trick for President Clinton was to receive credit or even to share credit with congressional Republicans for positive legislative achievements, while avoiding the blame for unpopular reductions in the growth of spending. By the time Congress recessed in August 1996, President Clinton had accomplished precisely those goals.

The Separated System

A separated system necessarily operates through a series of approximations. One of the casualties is the swift formulation and implementation of the best solution. Instead, the competition among institutions takes time. It fosters a melding toward the middling rather than the adoption of one or another version of perfection. And so critics who believe they know the answers—who are "right," in Schattschneider's terms—are understandably frustrated by a system in which they have access but over which they lack control.

At present, the agenda includes a series of basic questions on what government should do, on which government should do it, and on the capacity of the private sphere to solve public problems. This debate should not and will not be settled by one party or one institution—and surely not in a hundred days. Governing is real-life speculation. Some systems work with "clean" theories—the most pristine of which have been shown to be very wrong. The separated system is "unclean." It promotes access, propagates legitimacy, and disperses accountability, yet compels agreement. It cannot be made to work simply.

Acknowledgments

This chapter was prepared during the period I served as Douglas Dillon Visiting Fellow at the Brookings Institution. I wish to express my appreciation for that support (including a grant to Brookings from the Alcoa Foundation), as well as for the research assistance provided by Corey Cook, University of Wisconsin–Madison, and Laurel Imig, the Brookings Institution.

Notes

1. E.E. Schattschneider, *Two Hundred Million Americans in Search of a Government* (New York: Holt, Rinehart, and Winston, 1969), 53.

2. Lloyd N. Cutler, "To Form a Government," *Foreign Affairs* 59 (Fall 1980): 127–28.

3. Arend Lijphart, "Introduction," in *Parliamentary versus Presidential Government*, ed. Arend Lijphart (New York: Oxford University Press, 1992), 15.

4. David R. Mayhew, *Divided We Govern: Party Control, Lawmaking, and Investigations, 1946–1990* (New Haven: Yale University Press, 1991), 76.

Keith Krehbiel approaches this issue differently but with a similar conclusion, that "gridlock occurs in divided and unified government alike." "Institutional and Partisan Sources of Gridlock: A Theory of Divided and Unified Government," forthcoming in the *Journal of Theoretical Politics,* 1996. George C. Edwards III, Andrew Barrett, and Jeffrey Peake show that divided government has an impact on legislation that fails if the administration is in opposition. "The Legislative Impact of Divided Government: What *Failed* to Pass in Congress?" paper presented at the annual meeting of the American Political Science Association, Chicago, 1995.

5. T.R. Reid, "Japanese Coalition Parties Dealt Setback," *Washington Post,* 10 April 1995, A15.

6. Thomas E. Mann and Norman J. Ornstein make this point in a comment on Cutler's article, noting that "the recent deadlocks or failures of policy initiatives [that so concerned Cutler] have been as much failures of political will and skill as anything else." *Foreign Affairs* 59 (Winter 1980/1981): 418.

7. For example, in 1994 the Democrats held 56 percent of the Senate seats, yet had 63 percent of the one-third up for reelection (22 of 35 seats). Having the same ratio of seats held to those up for reelection is pure coincidence.

8. The count is based on who led the party either as Speaker or minority leader. Thus Sam Rayburn and Joseph Martin traded places twice in the immediate postwar period but served as principal leaders of their respective parties throughout.

9. It is also the case that most committee chairs previously served as major subcommittee chairs. As an extreme case, Jamie Whitten (D–Miss.) first served as an appropriations subcommittee chair in 1949, then the committee chair in 1979, finally stepping down in 1991.

10. The Republicans reduced staff and eliminated the Office of Technology Assessment when they won majority status in the 104th Congress.

11. An argument made in Charles O. Jones, "A Way of Life and Law," *American Political Science Review* 89 (March 1995): 1–9.

12. For details, see David Stockman, *The Triumph of Politics: Why the Reagan Revolution Failed* (New York: Harper & Row, 1986).

13. James L. Sundquist, ed., *Beyond Gridlock? Prospects for the Clinton Years and After* (Washington, D.C.: Brookings Institution, 1993), 25.

14. Estimates vary on how many Reagan-Bush voters chose Perot. One exit poll had 56 percent of Perot voters having voted for Bush in 1988 (17 percent for Dukakis). *American Enterprise,* January/February 1993, 94. A Democratic Leadership Council study found that "roughly 70 percent of those over age 30 ... supported either Ronald Reagan or Bush during the 1980s" (as reported in the *Washington Post,* 8 July 1993, A1). The National Election Study found that 24.3 percent of 1988 Bush voters chose Clinton in 1992, while 21.8 percent chose Perot. Herb Asher, "The Perot Campaign," in *Democracy's Feast: Elections in America,* ed. Herbert F. Weisberg (Chatham, N.J.: Chatham House, 1995), 171.

15. The evidence of success is actually rather limited. He did not receive a majority of the vote in any state, and it was Ross Perot's vote that surged at the end of the campaign, not Bill Clinton's. Further, in the 1994 election, Clinton campaigned vigorously during the final days, primarily along a northern tier of states. He visited nineteen places, making twenty-nine appearances. Republicans won all eight governor's races in these states (a net gain of three), as well as realizing a net gain of three Senate and sixteen House seats.

16. Private conversation.

17. Travel during this time is reported in detail in Charles O. Jones, "Campaigning to Govern: The Clinton Style," in *The Clinton Presidency: First Appraisals,* ed. Colin Campbell and Bert A. Rockman (Chatham, N.J.: Chatham House, 1996), 30–32.

18. As reported in Bob Woodward, *The Agenda: Inside the Clinton White House* (New York: Simon and Schuster, 1994), 141. Woodward offers evidence that the political consultants often won out over Howard Paster, the congressional liaison chief.

19. Mayhew's count for Clinton in the first year is seven: the deficit package, NAFTA, family leave, motor voter, national service, college loans, and the Brady bill. David R. Mayhew, "Clinton, the 103d Congress, and Unified Party Control: What Are the Lessons?" paper presented at a conference honoring Stanley Kelley Jr., Princeton University, 27–28 October 1995, table 3.

20. See Jones, "Campaigning to Govern," table 1.5, 32.

21. Helen Dewar et al., "Dust Clears on a Fruitful Legislative Year," *Washington Post,* 28 November 1993, A1.

22. Mayhew counts just four pieces of legislation. "Clinton, the 103d Congress," table 3.

23. "Perhaps the Worst Congress," *Washington Post,* 7 October 1994, A24. Others noted the return of gridlock. "Gridlock's Political Price," *New York Times,* 9 October 1994, 14.

24. Cited in Norman Ornstein, "The GOP Revolution," *Roll Call,* 11 September 1995, B38.

25. Calculated from votes listed in *Congressional Quarterly Weekly Report,* 8 April 1995, 1006.

26. *New York Times,* 28 September 1994, A20.

27. Charles O. Jones, *The Presidency in a Separated System* (Washington, D.C.: Brookings Institution, 1994), 1.

ALAN EHRENHALT

Mayor Daley and Modern Democracy:
What We Should Have Learned
from Chicago in the 1950s

I N 1975, AFTER a long but singularly uneventful career in Illinois politics, a round-faced Chicago tavern owner named John G. Fary was rewarded with a promotion to Congress. On the night of his election, at age sixty-four, he announced his agenda for everyone to hear. "I will go to Washington to help represent Mayor Daley," he declared. "For twenty-one years, I represented the mayor in the legislature, and he was always right."

Richard J. Daley died the next year, but Fary soon discovered the same qualities of infallibility in Thomas P. ("Tip") O'Neill, the U.S. House Speaker under whom he served. Over four congressional terms, he never cast a single vote against the Speaker's position on any issue of significance. From the leadership's point of view, Fary was an automatic yes.

And that, in a sense, was his undoing. Faced with a difficult primary challenge from an aggressive Chicago alderman, Fary had little to talk about other than his legendary willingness to do whatever he was told. The Chicago newspapers made sport of him. "Fary's lackluster record," one of them said, "forfeits his claim to a House seat." He was beaten badly and sent home to his tavern on the Southwest Side to ponder the troubling changes in modern political life.

It was not an easy thing for him to understand. The one principle John Fary had stood for over thirty years in politics—obedience— had come into obvious disrepute. The legislator who simply followed the rules as they came down to him invited open ridicule as a mindless hack.

The "Old Politics"

No quality is less attractive in American politics these days than obedience—not foolishness or deceit or even blatant corruption. There is no one of whom we are more scornful than the officeholder who refuses to make choices for himself. There are bumper stickers all over Washington that say, in big block capital letters, QUESTION AUTHORITY. There are none that say LISTEN TO THE BOSS.

John Fary made a career out of listening to the boss. Of course, he did not have much alternative. In the Chicago politics of the 1950s, you could either be part of the machine and entertain a realistic hope of holding office, or be against it and have virtually no hope at all. Fary actually began as something of an upstart. In 1951 he ran in the Twelfth Ward as a challenger to the Swinarski family, which more or less dominated ward politics in alliance with other machine lieutenants. After that unsuccessful experience, however, Fary made his accommodations to the system; he had no other choice.[1]

If Fary ever chafed at the rules of his constricted political world, he never did so in public. He seemed content voting with the leadership, gratified to be part of an ordered political system, content working behind the bar at his tavern when he was not practicing politics in Springfield or Washington. He did not appear to give much thought to the possibility of doing it any other way. When he achieved passage of the one notable legislative initiative of his long career, a state law legalizing Bingo, he celebrated by inventing a new drink called "Bingo Bourbon" and serving it to his customers on the house.

One thing we can say fairly confidently about the political system in Chicago in the 1950s is that it did not offer most participants a great deal of choice. There were always a few people on the city council who served out careers as mavericks and gadflies and got a lot of press coverage for being the anti-Daley bloc. But there were only a handful of wards that would tolerate that sort of behavior. For the most part, the only practical way to have a career was to sign up with the Daley machine and hang on for dear life, as John Fary did.

And that is not too bad a description of the way politics worked in most of America in the 1950s, at most of its levels of operation. It was true of most legislatures. If you wanted a political career in a county in South Carolina—let us say you wanted to be a member of the state legislature—you applied to your state senator and asked for instructions. The state senate essentially was the government in South Carolina in those days, not only the state government but the local government too. The state senators told everybody what to do. Or in Connecticut, the people that really mattered were the unelected chairmen of the state Democratic and Republican parties. They controlled all the decisions.

And so to be a rank-and-file state representative in South Carolina, or in Connecticut, or in most states for that matter, was to be a little like our friend John Fary in Chicago: a spectator. I am fascinated by the statistics. In 1951, in the Connecticut House of Representatives, the combined number of votes cast by members of the Democratic Party against the party's majority position was zero. Nobody voted against the party line all year. The chairman told them what to do, and they did it. This was a deference to authority that very few legislative bodies even in a parliamentary system would have been able to match.

Or here is an interesting one. On the Chicago City Council, in the Daley years, the mayor not only was the presiding officer but had control of the microphone that amplified what the aldermen were saying. If the mayor did not like something an alderman said, he had the prerogative of just shutting off the sound and forcing him to shout or else not be heard by anybody more than a few feet away. And I do not know of anybody who claimed there was anything outrageous about this, other than the people who had it done to them.

When authority did not take the form of deference to an individual, as it did in the Chicago of Mayor Daley, it often took the form of deference to a small knot of insiders who met in a restaurant somewhere and made all the important decisions of the city council or the legislature. I have always been struck by the importance of restaurants as a primary institution of American politics in those years. Whatever community or state capital you go to, you learn that in those days, a group of men sat around over breakfast or lunch and did the real work that the legislative body later ratified.

In Utica, New York, for example, a city I spent some time looking at, there was an Italian restaurant called Marino's, with the old-fashioned sort of wooden booths with high backs. The town political boss, Rufus Elefante, used to have lunch there every day, and all of Elefante's boys were there. They arranged themselves in different booths, and if you went in there as a customer, the booth you went to depended on the favor you wanted done—one booth was for construction permits, one for jobs in city hall, that sort of thing. This was the effective seat of government in this city of 100,000 people. And if you needed something really important, you would go straight to the back room, get into a card game with some of the boys, and lose as much money as possible very quickly. Then you would have a good chance of getting what you needed.

In Sioux Falls, South Dakota, another place I studied, it all happened over breakfast rather than lunch. If you were an up-and-coming young man and wanted to get somewhere in politics, the thing to do was to stop in for coffee in the morning about ten o'clock at Kirk's café and try to make conversation with some of the realtors and insurance men and other businessmen who gathered there every morning. This was the nomination process in Sioux Falls, and in a good many other midwestern towns in that era. The boys would sit around a table in Kirk's and decide who should be mayor, who should be the city commissioners.

Now in the 1950s, as in the present, a young person with the determination to make his way in politics had a reasonable chance to do it. He had to be male—that is one important difference. But there were opportunities to get ahead. One generation was always yielding gradually to the pressures of another. Hard work helped you get ahead. But in those days, unlike these, a lot of this hard work consisted of deference to authority.

That does not necessarily mean literal obedience to command. If you made your way onto the Chicago City Council with machine sponsorship, or into the South Carolina legislature under the umbrella of the state senator, you pretty much knew what was wanted. You did not have to be given orders every day. You knew the relationship between going along and staying in office. And more important, it is unlikely, if you were John Fary on the Chicago City Council, that you wanted anything much that the boss did not want. You thought along the same lines. That was one reason you were there.

Of course, any political system produces its occasional frustrations, resentments, and rebellions. No legislator and certainly no legislative body was under anybody's thumb 100 percent of the time. But the norm was deference. Whatever part of the country we are talking about, whatever level of the political system, saying no was a demonstration of individualism that one did not undertake lightly.

So, it was a system in which authority existed and was exercised in a very clear way. I want to stress one other point: it was a system in which corruption was simply a fact of life. As the boss of the city of Utica said in the 1950s, after a series of reports came out documenting that prostitution and gambling were rampant in that community and that the boss himself was making money selling tires to the city at higher than market price, "We believe that government must be tolerant of human weakness." That's the way the whole system was in the 1950s—profoundly tolerant of human weakness.

Let me go back and illustrate some of that by making reference to Chicago and the world of Mayor Daley.

Traditional Politics and Original Sin

There are many ways to think about Richard J. Daley, who was one of the most interesting characters, it seems to me, in modern American politics, serving as mayor of Chicago for twenty-one years, from 1955 to 1976.[2] Most common is the "Boss" Daley stereotype, the legend of the mayor who may or may not have stolen the 1960 presidential election for John Kennedy, and whose police beat up antiwar protesters at the Democratic convention in 1968. There is also the Mayor

Daley who was quite genuinely a reformer of Chicago government in his first two terms in the 1950s and early 1960s.

But in trying to understand the Chicago politics of those days, I like to refer to Richard J. Daley as a manager of sin, that is, a decision maker who accepted the reality of sinful citizens and constant temptation, tolerated them up to a point, even took advantage of their presence to keep an organization functioning, but did his best to control the level of misdeeds and to keep them from taking over and breeding chaos. When he first ran for mayor in 1955, the *Chicago Tribune,* which was very much against Daley, wrote that he was the candidate of the hoodlum element. Daley's response was this: "I would not unleash the forces of evil."

I think that was very revealing. Daley did not claim to be unaware that evil was loose in Chicago or that he had no contact with it. He merely promised to keep it on a leash. In the Chicago of those days, if you were stopped for speeding, the expectation was that you would simply slip the arresting officer $10, and he would forget about it. If you wanted to build a driveway alongside your house, you had to pay off an alderman. Daley, by the way, actually put a stop to the practice of aldermen selling driveway permits. But it lasted into the late 1950s.

A Chicago resident who made a visit to a county courtroom in those days frequently saw campaign posters bearing the name and likeness of the judge who was presiding there. Bailiffs handed out campaign literature to the families of defendants. At the precinct level, on election day, it was not unusual to have precinct captains, the foot soldiers of the Daley organization, walk right into a voting booth with the voter and assist the person in making sure the vote was cast the correct way. All of this existed in the midst of what was really quite an innovative and competent city government. Daley was an experienced financial manager who kept a close watch on city budgets, an administrator who reorganized whole areas of the bureaucracy and got them functioning better, a builder who brought some life to downtown development for the first time in twenty years.

And yet there was no denying that sin, or at least perceived sin, flourished in the 1950s under the protection of the political regime. There were the illegal dice games in the back rooms of restaurants; there were B-girl joints, essentially taverns where prostitutes operated by sanction of the local police captain. There was the somewhat shadowy presence of the Mafia on the fringes of the whole business community and political system. In 1957, with Daley's blessing, the Chicago Democrats slated for Congress a man named Roland Libonati, who was perhaps best known for a photograph of him and Al Capone enjoying a day at the baseball game together in the 1930s. Libonati's answer to that was to say that "guilt by association don't go in my area." As it evidently didn't in Daley's.

One has to presume that Daley did not consider slating Libonati to be a violation of his earlier promise "not to unleash the forces of evil" on Chicago. Either the election of a *Mafioso* to Congress failed to meet the test of evil, in Daley's view, or else adding him to the existing delegation was an event whose consequences were too trivial to bother fighting. Or perhaps the mayor felt he was improving the moral climate of his own city by shipping Libonati off to Washington.

What is indisputable is that Daley was a man who thought about good and evil, who absorbed strict standards of right and wrong from his religious upbringing and applied them to the people he dealt with in personal life. He was not a teetotaller, but he did not like drunkenness, and he did not like profanity. Two of his three rules of public speaking were "Never speak with liquor on your breath" and "Don't tell dirty jokes." (The third was "Sit down after five minutes.") But what bothered Daley more than anything was womanizing. "If one of his aides or hand-picked officeholders is shacking up with a woman, he will know it," Mike Royko wrote of Daley. "And if that man is married and a Catholic, his career will wither and die."

Nearly everyone who has written about Daley in his lifetime and since has been struck by the fundamental incongruity of a man who was sincerely troubled by the language, drinking habits, and marital infidelities of those around him—and yet, for all his efforts to create a "modern" and "respectable" political machine, still permitted massive corruption to persist. Daley's own floor leader in the city council was buying land on inside information and selling it at huge profits; his press secretary was soliciting bribes from people who wanted construction contracts at the airport.

Decades later, it should be safe to venture the final judgment that Daley himself was not doing any of these things. Millions of dollars and years of effort were spent by both press and prosecutors to investigate the possibility that Daley was corrupt, and not a shred of evidence was ever produced. As Eugene Kennedy wrote, "he entered the slaughterhouse every day, but he ducked the spraying blood."

Yet it is also impossible to believe that Daley did not know about all the corruption going on around him. What can most truthfully be said about him is that he was a manager of corruption and a manager of sin. He accepted its existence, accepted it as part of life, and saw it

ALAN EHRENHALT

as the responsibility of a leader to keep it under control, or if that was impossible, at least to keep it out of sight. One can say of Daley and of Chicago that they were living under the domination of a very Catholic view of life: the best one can do with the endless parade of human weakness is to live as well as possible in its midst.

So, what are some things we can say about American politics in the 1950s, in Chicago and all over America?[3] One is that, for most of the people who chose to participate in it, it offered relatively little choice or freedom of operation. It required a great deal of deference to figures of authority, whether they happened to be the mayor who could turn off your microphone at the city council or the state party chairman who would see that you did not get renominated to the legislature if you voted the wrong way. Another is that it featured little knots of power, little subcommunities like the ones that met in restaurants for breakfast or lunch, that made the real decisions, without much public scrutiny or participation by rank-and-file elected officials. And finally, it was a system that lived with a lot of sin, a lot of corruption and personal misbehavior, and in which most people felt that you did not *eradicate* sin from public affairs; you tried to keep it under control as best you could and get things done around it.

The "New Politics"

Let us look briefly at how some of this has changed. I do not think I am saying anything very controversial if I tell you that in American politics in the 1990s there is a great deal of choice. Anybody starting a career at almost any level is not faced with problems of having to defer to authority: he or she confronts problems of how to express independence and individuality in a way that is appealing to the electorate. We have pretty much a system of independent actors. Merely to get elected is to occupy a position of at least potential political influence, in a way that simply was not true in the 1950s. I talked about this a lot a few years ago in my book *The United States of Ambition*.[4] I do not want to dwell on that, but I do not think anything has happened since then to make it less true. If anything, it is more true.

The Chicago City Council is an example. Today the mayor of Chicago is Richard M. Daley, son of the legendary Richard J. Daley, and he confronts a completely different situation: a council of fifty individualistic aldermen that he pretty much has to court on a one-by-one basis, threading his way around the multitude of factions and ethnic groupings that govern the place. There is no shutting off somebody's microphone to silence him, as there was in his father's day; there is no threatening people by telling them they are going to be denied renomination if they do not behave. The modern Mayor Daley lacks those tools of authority. The remarkable thing is that he has managed to keep the city government together pretty well anyway, and he has been a rather popular mayor. But I think he has been the exception rather than the rule.

More typical, I am afraid, is a place like Dallas. It never possessed a party machine, as Chicago did. But it had the Citizens Council, a close-knit group of about 200 business executives, and this council pretty much handpicked the elected officials and managers. As a prominent Dallas politician once said, "You get the banks, the utilities, then insurance, the big stores, and the papers. Once you got them, you don't need anybody else." In the mid-1960s, when the city's mayor decided Dallas needed a set of goals to propel it into the future, he appointed a committee of eighty-seven people, whisked them out of town for a three-day retreat, and came home with what turned out to be most of the city's governmental agenda for a decade to come. Those eighty-seven people were the voice of local authority; they spoke for Dallas.

Today, no one does. Dallas is governed, if that is the word, by a city council of fourteen members, each representing a different faction and bickering endlessly in its behalf, along with a mayor who struggles helplessly to impose some discipline or even keep the noise down.

By and large, this sort of thing has been happening in state politics as well. In 1995 I was struck by what went on in Virginia, which had always been a symbol of decorum and civility in politics, and of deference to the governor at least on a personal level. And a place where tradition was honored. You know the story about how many legislators it takes to change a light bulb in Virginia? The answer is two—one to put in the new bulb, and one to say what a fine light bulb the old one really was.

Well, all that seemed to break down in Virginia in 1995. The legislature and the governor fought and called each other names, and the legislature adjourned rather than let the governor come over and give his State of the State address. So he had to give the speech in his office, with only the television cameras for an audience. The norm in Virginia politics, at least for the moment, had become mutual disrespect.

It is true that this is not happening everywhere. There are states, just as there are cities, where mayors and governors are doing fine and getting what they want out of legislative bodies and maintaining their popularity. But I would argue that in the 1990s the norm is disrespect, and it takes a substantial effort to overcome it.[5] You can argue that making a political executive earn respect and authority is not such a bad idea. I am not arguing that for the moment. I am saying that not too long ago it was the other way around: the norm was deference, and you had to earn disrespect by misbehaving.

In that context, we should look at Congress for a few paragraphs. Over the past decade, there has been no better model for rising political incivility than the U.S. Congress, with the two parties exchanging insults and the Republican minority lobbing grenades at the Democratic leadership in a way that simply had not happened before. Starting in 1995 we had the chief bomb thrower in the position of authority himself, in the person of Newt Gingrich, the Speaker of the House. Remarkably enough, given authority, he became something of an authoritarian, dictating the committee assignments and chairmanships and dictating that his mostly very new and young Republican majority vote as he himself and his "Contract with America" demanded. And generally he was getting away with this.

What did this mean? Was it a turning of the corner, as even the most antiauthoritarian forces in politics began to recognize some need for order and discipline in the legislative process? Or was it an aberrational moment, based on the euphoria of sudden Republican control, certain to dissipate into the more typical squabbling and refusal of the rank and file to remain in step? I do not know the answer to this.

But whatever happens to authority in the Congress, there are some long-term changes in congressional life that I think are simply going to continue. One is the erosion of Congress as a community of people who spend a lot of time with each other and get to know one another well. People still write articles about the U.S. Senate as a clubby institution. But the reality is that it has not been like that for the past twenty years, if in fact it ever was. It is, instead, a place where individual senators race around frantically, to fulfill the demands of the daily schedules they carry around printed on file cards, and scarcely get time in the course of such a day to say hello to each other, let alone become boon companions. This too is something I wrote about at some length in the *United States of Ambition,* and I shall not dwell on it now.

I do want to point out one way in which this has been mirrored in state politics in the past decade or so. I talked earlier about the café in local politics as the sort of center of a subcommunity of insiders who made the important decisions on a city council or a county commission back in the 1950s. At the state level there was something rather comparable, and this was the "watering hole," the bar in the state capital town where the legislators went at the end of the day, where plots were hatched and sins occasionally concocted, but also where members of a government developed the social familiarity and fellowship that allowed decisions to be made and work to get done.

So, if you were a legislator in New Mexico, you went to a place called the Bull Ring. Or there was the Broken Spoke in Austin, Texas; or Clyde's, in Tallahassee, the Florida capital; or any of several dozen places that fulfilled this function. They were symbols of the community feeling that existed in any American legislature a generation ago.

But everyone in state politics will tell you that they have been dying out in the past couple of decades. The reasons are several. For one thing, there just is not as much alcohol consumed by politicians as there used to be. In many states, legislators did not have offices in the old days, so they had to find some place to do business, and a tavern served that function. Also, as sessions get longer, more members bring their families to the capital, so there is not the feeling of bachelors on holiday that used to surround pretty much any legislator. And the rules are generally tougher on what legislators can accept as gifts from lobbyists, so the incentive to hang out and get a lobbyist to buy you drinks and dinner is not what it once was.

Maybe most important, you are dealing with a more serious generation of people for the most part, people who are more likely to continue their regular work schedule on into the evening than to spend it shooting the breeze with colleagues at a bar. But the upshot of all this is that state legislators, like members of Congress, often do not know each other the way they once did. And if this has prevented some chicanery and some embarrassing cronyism from taking place, it also had had some obvious effects on the level of civility and the sense of teamwork in a legislative body.

As long as we are talking about drinking and bars, let me return to the question of sin in politics. It seems to me that we have moved from a world in which there was considerable corruption at all levels, and in which the people in charge had the task of managing it, to one in which there is an official policy of zero tolerance, encouraged by the scrutiny of the media. That situation leads us to a whole raft of bizarre consequences.

I offer as my one exhibit on this issue the indictment and conviction of Dan Rostenkowski. The former chairman of the Ways and Means Committee in the House of Representatives faced seventeen corruption charges, which essentially revolved around two accusations: one, that he placed people on his payroll who did not do very much work, and two, that he took some of his official postage-stamp allotment and converted it to cash, in violation of House rules.

I do not quite know what to say about such a bill of particulars. I admit to being influenced by my feeling that Rostenkowski, who by the way was a protégé of the late Mayor Daley, was, over his last decade in Congress, quite a good public servant. But I guess what I would say ultimately is this: We have so lost our sense of what sin is in politics that we apply rigid and bizarre formulas that have nothing to do with the actual notion of harm or even moral transgression. We have lost our sense of proportion about sin primarily because we have lost our sense of sin itself.

Political Change and Cultural Shift

And this brings me to the one point on which I hope I can convince you: we have trouble knowing what sin is in politics because we have lost our sense of it in the society at large. And something similar can be said about all the topics I have been discussing. There has been an erosion of authority in American politics in the past generation precisely in the way that there has been an erosion of it in the society.

Legislatures do not have the community feeling of small towns the way they once did, because small towns do not have it either. There has been a profusion of choice for the young politician, just as there is a bewildering profusion of choices placed in front of us in our lives every day. In other words, at least at this one time in this place, America at the end of the twentieth century, most of the important political questions are really cultural questions. Politics reflect the culture and the society of the times, rather than shaping it.

In the past generation, we have moved whole areas of life, large and small, out of the realm of permanence and authority and into the realm of change and choice. We have gained the psychological freedom to ask ourselves at any moment not only whether we are eating the right cereal but whether we are in the right neighborhood, the right job, the right relationship. Our daily lives are monuments to selection, and to making for ourselves decisions that someone above us used to make on our behalf.

Americans breakfast on choice (sometimes on products literally named for it). They come home to a television set that offers so many choices the newspaper cannot devise a grid to show them all. We believe in choice, many of us, as the answer to problems of education. We use the word when we are really talking about abortion. We are just a society that, in this particular stage of its life, is fond of the idea.

In contrast, we do not like the idea of authority very much. To most Americans of the baby-boom generation, authority will always be a word with sinister connotations, calling forth a rush of uncomfortable memories about the schools, churches, and families in which baby boomers grew up. Rebellion against those memories constituted the defining event of their generational lives. Wherever on the political spectrum this generation has landed, it has brought its suspicion of authority with it. "Authority," says P.J. O'Rourke, speaking for his baby-boom cohort loud and clear, "has always attracted the lowest elements in the human race."[6]

You can comb the shelves of any bookstore crowded with volumes on corporate management without coming across one that defends the old-fashioned pyramid, in which orders come down from the chief executive, military style, and descend intact to the lower reaches of the organization. There are corporations that still operate that way, but they are regarded as dinosaurs; corporate hierarchies are out of fashion. The literature is all about constructing management out of webs rather than pyramids, about decentralizing the decision process, empowering people at all levels of the organization. The words "command and control" are the obscenities of present-day management writing.

As they are, more broadly, in economic thinking. Five years ago, few Americans were familiar with the phrase "command economy." Now, virtually all of us know what it means. It is the definition of a society that fails because it attempts to make economic decisions by hierarchy rather than by the free choice of its individual citizens. It is the most broadly agreed upon reason for the abject failure of world communism. The communist implosion both reinforced and seemed to validate our generational suspicions about hierarchy and authority in all their manifestations, foreign and domestic—the American CEOs and school principals of the 1950s almost as much as the dictators who made life miserable in authoritarian countries around the world.

It is, quite simply, the ideology of the baby-boom generation, which is my generation—and Bill Clinton's, by the way; he is five months older than I am—that choice is something good and authority is something bad. I know the extent to which I am oversimplifying and the number of counterexamples that will probably come to mind, but I think the principle is right. And I think it explains a good deal of what has happened in politics in the past decade or so, just as it explains a lot of what has happened in the larger precincts of the society.

This is not an original idea with me. Other people have been saying something related to it for quite a long time. Michael Barone made the point a couple of years ago that incoming American presidents do not so much generate change as ratify it.[7] What has sometimes been called the "Reagan revolution" in American government, to the extent you can call it a revolution, reflected suspicions about government—and I would say about authority itself—that had been brewing for more than a decade at that time, on the left as well as the right in American politics.

Indeed, if there is one thing the left and the right have agreed on in American politics since roughly 1965—the formative time of the baby-boom generation—it is the illegitimacy of traditional authority as it existed during our generational youth. Anything that has taken place in politics since then has taken place within the context of that idea, which I would insist is generational and cultural, rather than purely ideological or political.

If all this seems something of a commonplace, I would insist that it does have implications that we do not always face up to. One is that our attempts to reform the American political system from within, no matter how thoughtful and well intentioned they may be, are likely to have a low percentage of succeeding. If the problem is not within the political system but outside it, it probably cannot be fixed from the inside.

Think for a moment about the presidential nominating process. What are the common complaints against it? That it throws up a raft of candidates whose only reason for being there is their own ambition, who represent nobody beyond themselves, whom we really know very little about, who spend a year or more raising huge sums of money and then exhibit themselves in the most demeaning spectacle of self-promotion, one that tests their physical stamina but offers scarcely a clue to whether they would be any good as the chief executive of the country. It gives us such people as Gary Hart, odd sorts of characters with no ties to any organized interest in the political system, who pride themselves on being untethered individualists.

In short, we have a system of self-nomination for president, just as we do for most of the offices further down the ladder. We lack any sort of screening process that would bring people forward as standard-bearers for factions or interests, rather than as freelance individualists. And so we debate ways to change this system to make it more orderly, more comprehensible to the average voter, more capable of bringing out the best potential talent, better fitted to the qualities we are actually looking for in a president, as opposed to just a candidate. And we have made very little progress along these lines—if anything, the process is worse than it was twenty years ago.

I would merely argue that in its individualism, its openness, its lack of deference to authority, its offering a profusion of choices rather than a structured decision, the presidential nominating system has been very good at reflecting values in broader American society over the past twenty years. We may not like it when we see it, but it does look like America, to use a phrase that was popular not too long ago. And the most sensible thing to say about it is that it will change when the values underpinning it begin to change—probably not until then.

In making what may seem to be a sweeping statement about politics reflecting culture and values, and not the other way around, I do not mean to make a hard-and-fast rule about all times and all places. There are obviously many similarities between life in America and life in Britain in the 1990s, or life in any of the advanced Western democracies. And yet the qualities of authority and deference that have been lost in American politics during the past couple of decades remain clearly stronger in Britain—to become an MP, for example, or to succeed as an MP, still requires a great deal more deference to leadership and passage through a screening process than is true in the United States. One has to be very careful in drawing such parallels, for there are obviously political rules within any country that help to maintain their importance regardless of social change.

Nor would I argue, for that matter, that you can never make great political change just by tinkering with the rules. Reapportionment in all the legislative bodies of American government—the redrawing of districts to make them equal in population—has been a cataclysmic change that was essentially technical in nature. Clearly, it had some relation to the growing emphasis on equality in the larger society. But in essence it was an effort to fix a real flaw in the system from inside, and it did what it was meant to do. So you can sometimes change things that way.

I would argue, however, that in general we try to answer too many questions about politics from within the political system, when the first thing we should be doing is asking how that system reflects our present-day culture and values. And whether there really are solutions inside the system or whether the solutions, if there are any, lie in gradually changing broader values. Will the next generation, my children's generation coming to maturity in the first decade of the next century, feel itself drawn toward values that were essentially missing in its childhood years: a belief in authority and deference, a turning away from the glorification of choice in favor of habit and custom? Will it be drawn toward a more traditional view of right and wrong and a rediscovery of the notion of sin as a fact of everyday life?

The truth is that I do not know whether any of these things will happen. What I do predict is that when and if these things happen in American society, they will happen in American politics, and probably not before.

Notes

1. Details on the career of John G. Fary can be found in *Congressional Quarterly Weekly Report*, 3 April 1982, 779; *Governing Magazine*, August 1992, 6; and his obituary in the *Chicago Tribune*, 8 June 1984. See also Alan Ehrenhalt, *The Lost City: Discovering the Forgotten Virtues of Community in the Chicago of the 1950s* (New York: Basic Books, 1995).

2. For biographical detail on Richard J. Daley, see Bill Gleason, *Daley of Chicago* (New York: Simon and Schuster, 1970); Mike Royko, *Boss: Richard J. Daley of Chicago* (New York: New American Library, 1971); Len O'Connor, *Clout: Mayor Daley and His City* (New York: Avon Books, 1976); and Eugene C. Kennedy, *Himself! The Life and Times of Richard J. Daley* (New York: Viking Press, 1978).

3. For perhaps the best survey of American politics in this period, see D.W. Brogan, *An Introduction to American Politics* (New York: Harper & Brothers, 1954).

4. Alan Ehrenhalt, *The United States of Ambition: Politicians, Power, and the Pursuit of Office* (New York: Times Books, 1991).

5. Ibid., 27–29; see also *Governing Magazine*, July 1991, 13.

6. P.J. O'Rourke, *Parliament of Whores: A Lone Humorist Attempts to Explain the Entire U.S. Government* (New York: Atlantic Monthly Press, 1991), 233.

7. Michael Barone, *Our Country: The Shaping of America from Roosevelt to Reagan* (New York: Free Press, 1990).

ISSUES

EDWARD G. CARMINES

AND

GEOFFREY C. LAYMAN

Issue Evolution
in Postwar American Politics:
Old Certainties and Fresh Tensions

T HE POSTWAR PERIOD has seen significant changes in American politics. In Congress, the power of committee chairmen, once the barons of the congressional universe, has been reduced and that of party leaders restored. Congressional accommodation and compromise have given way to fierce partisanship and floor proceedings often filled with rancor and personal attacks. The president, once seen as the leader of his party, now stands above party, speaking directly to the American people through the mass media, especially television. And the nomination of presidential candidates has become an exercise in mass democracy with the growth of presidential primaries, whereas just several decades ago a small group of national and state party leaders dominated the process.

These are only a few of the many changes that have transformed American politics during the last half century. In this chapter we focus on a phenomenon that is no less important to America's changing political universe but has received relatively little attention: the expansion of the nation's issue agenda.[1] At the close of World War II, American politics revolved around the social welfare issues associated with the New Deal. Democrats were committed to the idea of an activist role for government in managing the economy and providing for the general welfare, whereas Republicans stood in opposition to this role for government. While partisan disagreement has continued along this broad ideological dimension, two new clusters of issues have emerged in American politics during the postwar period.

The first major issue to affect American politics in the post–New Deal period was race: specifically, the extension of equal rights to black Americans. FDR had skillfully avoided issues of race throughout his presidency. But beginning in the Truman administration in the late 1940s and culminating in the Kennedy/Johnson years, race became a powerful and divisive issue in American politics, especially disruptive to the New Deal Democratic coalition. The 1960s saw another issue conflict arise in American politics. Initially spawned by the civil rights and anti–Vietnam war movements, this conflict became focused on social and cultural issues such as the treatment of gays, the role of women, and most important, abortion. Racial issues had been far more disruptive to the Democratic Party than the Republican Party, but social issues affected both parties, the GOP more recently.

The purpose of this chapter is to trace the evolution of these three broad clusters of domestic issues in the postwar period. We begin with a brief overview of issue evolution during this period. Then, after discussing measures for these issue dimensions, we examine interparty differences along these issues over the past five decades. We next consider the changes in social-group bases of the party coalitions and show that these changes are linked to the emergence of new issue dimensions in American politics. Finally, we examine divisions *within* the party coalitions, divisions associated with social welfare, racial, and social and cultural issues.

A Historical Overview

The end of World War II saw Americans struggling with essentially the same set of issues that had dominated the country since the Great Depression. The specifics were many, but they all boiled down to a single question: what was the proper role of government, notably the national government, in providing for the general welfare of the citizenry? Initially, this question was answered in the context of the Great Depression. Republican President Herbert Hoover had responded tepidly to the economic collapse, still hoping the market economy would right itself and leaving more decisive action to the states. Roosevelt ran an equally cautious presidential election campaign in 1932, but on taking office, he quickly moved to take strong action.

From labor legislation to Social Security to progressive taxation, Roosevelt committed the Democratic Party—and through it, the country—to governmental activism on matters of social welfare. If rural areas lacked electricity, the answer was the Tennessee Valley Authority; if the elderly lacked retirement funds, the answer was Social Security; if labor was unable to represent workers, the answer was the National Labor Relations Board. And so on. For every public problem, there seemed to be a governmental solution. Not surprisingly, FDR's Democratic Party gained its most full-fledged support from groups that had been most adversely affected by the Great Depression. Those of lower status and modest incomes, including the unemployed, unskilled workers, northern blacks, and ethnic and religious minorities became the core groups in the New Deal Democratic coalition, along with white southerners who had been solidly Democratic since the Civil War.

On virtually every issue, the minority Republicans opposed Democratic social welfare initiatives. They stood for limited government, unconstrained capitalism, and an Anglo-Saxon America. Their core support came from high-income earners and upper-status citizens, along with white Protestants residing outside the South. Thus for three decades after the Great Depression, the New Deal party system was a stable alignment and had a stable winner. Democrats were the majority party as long as elections were fought over the social welfare issues associated with the New Deal.

This simple equilibrium, however, could not withstand the introduction of racial issues into national politics. The first signs of the breakup of the New Deal Democratic majority were seen in the 1948 presidential election, when a group of southern Democrats—upset with the party's adoption of a modest civil rights plank—bolted the national party convention and ran a separate third-party presidential campaign. As the civil rights movement gained momentum in the 1950s and early 1960s, it became clear that the New Deal Democratic coalition could not remain intact. The reason was obvious: the party included two groups, southern whites and blacks, that held diametrically opposed views on civil rights.

President Kennedy tried to straddle the racial divide, but by 1963 this was no longer possible. In June of that year, he finally sent a strong civil rights bill to Congress, and Johnson pressed successfully for its passage in the aftermath of Kennedy's assassination. The 1964 presidential election confirmed this reorientation of the party system; a liberal, prointegrationist Johnson was opposed by Republican nominee Barry Goldwater, one of the few senators outside the South to vote against the Civil Rights Act of 1964. Thus racial issues transformed the original party alignment of the New Deal by providing an opening to Republicans among the party's racial right, notably southern whites but also lower-status northerners, and at the same time leading blacks to become the most loyal group in the *post*–New Deal Democratic coalition.

The incorporation of social and cultural issues into contemporary American politics then had a more diverse and complicated history. Originally associated with the New Left, these issues became part of the rebellion directed, not against modern conservatism, but against the liberal establishment of the 1950s and 1960s. As E.J. Dionne Jr. has observed, the New Left saw Vietnam as liberalism's war. As a result, " ... the New Left turned ferociously on the liberals and nearly all their works. The Great Society was condemned as 'the Great Barbecue.' Liberal tolerance was called 'repressive tolerance.' Liberalism became 'corporate liberalism.' "[2]

Adopting the stance of a counterculture, the New Left sought a freer lifestyle on a whole host of issues: abortion, drugs, relations between the sexes, the treatment of gays. Even as the New Left attacked modern liberalism and the Democratic Party, it fostered movements within the party that challenged liberal orthodoxy. In 1968, the anti-war presidential nominating campaigns of Robert Kennedy and Eugene McCarthy first brought elements of the New Left into the Democratic Party. In 1972, the nomination of George McGovern confirmed the influence not just of the antiwar forces but of a variety of left-oriented protest movements. Groups representing gays, feminists, and the young demanded—and received—a seat at the Democratic table. Once the target of the New Left, the Democratic Party of McGovern became identified with some of its most notable slogans, including the infamous three As: "acid, amnesty, and abortion."

As the Democratic Party moved left on social and cultural matters, the GOP became more attractive to opponents of this "new" morality. Once dominated by big business and Main Street, the GOP saw the influence of the cultural and religious right grow dramatically in the 1970s and 1980s. Takeover efforts were spearheaded by Jerry Falwell's Moral Majority, a coalition of groups and individuals formed to fight what they considered to be the moral decay of America. Their resentments ran far and deep. They opposed the Equal Rights Amendment, supported prayer in public schools, and, most important, opposed abortion totally. Their moral fundamentalism offended many traditional conservatives and moderates in the GOP, but increasingly the party was being remade in the image of the religious right.

This process reached perhaps its pinnacle at the 1992 GOP convention when Pat Buchanan gave a prime-time speech calling for a cultural civil war in America. And there was no doubt whatsoever which side he thought the Republican Party should be on. But the GOP remained divided on social and cultural issues, as moderates and economic conservatives called for the party to take softer stands on these divisive matters. Thus social and cultural issues—which earlier Republicans had used so skillfully to undermine the post–New Deal Democratic Party—now turned on them, undermining GOP efforts to build a permanent presidential majority.

This brief historical overview suggests that the expansion of the issue agenda was a notable feature of postwar American politics. We now turn to an examination of systematic evidence that focuses on issue evolution in this period.

Uncovering the Three Issue Dimensions

Our discussion identifies three distinct attitudinal dimensions of domestic policy in the United States in the postwar era: attitudes toward economic and social welfare issues, such as government spending and governmental responsibility to provide for the welfare of the citizenry; attitudes toward racial issues, such as desegregation and affirmative action; and attitudes toward social and cultural issues, such as abortion, women's rights, and homosexuals' rights. We examine partisan change over time on these three issue dimensions using the presidential year surveys of the American National Election Studies from 1956 through 1992. All of these studies include questions regarding attitudes toward social welfare and racial issues. All of the studies from 1972 through 1992 contain questions about social and cultural issues.

In order to determine if three distinct attitudinal dimensions concerning issues of American domestic policy in fact have existed throughout this period, we subjected the indicators for all of the major domestic issues in each study to a factor analysis. (A discussion of these analyses and their results is presented in appendix A). Since social and cultural issues were not included in the National Election Studies until 1972, we expect the analyses for the 1956–68 period to uncover only two attitudinal dimensions: attitudes toward racial issues and attitudes toward social welfare issues. As appendix A shows, this is indeed the case. Two dimensions emerge for the analyses in these years, with attitudes toward racial issues (such as school integration, housing integration, fair employment practices, and the pace of the civil rights movement) clustering on one, and opinions on social welfare issues (such as governmental responsibility to guarantee jobs to its citizens, a governmental role in providing medical services, and governmental aid to education) clustering strongly on the other.

Beginning with the introduction of cultural issues to the National Election Studies in 1972, our analyses should uncover three distinct attitudinal dimensions. As the results in appendix A make plain, this is also the case. Three dimensions emerge for each of the years from 1972 through 1992, with attitudes toward social welfare and economic issues loading strongly on one; attitudes toward civil rights and affirmative action loading strongly on another; and attitudes toward social and cultural issues (such as abortion, women's rights, homosexuals' rights, and prayer in the public schools) loading strongly on a third.[3]

Partisan Changes along the Three Issue Dimensions

The first question to ask about partisan change over this period concerns the positions of the parties on these issue dimensions. Has there been partisan change over time? Have the parties become more or less distinct? Figure 5.1 shows the mean positions of Democratic and Republican identifiers on social welfare issues from 1956 to 1992. As past research indicates, the mass party coalitions were already polarized along the social welfare dimension by 1956. In contrast to research showing no partisan change on social welfare issues after the 1950s, however, this figure demonstrates a steady, if not overwhelming, *growth* in the division of the party coalitions along the lines of social welfare issues after the mid-1970s. Sundquist argues that the presidency of Ronald Reagan actually brought about a revitalization of the social welfare cleavage in American politics, as Reagan propelled the Republican Party toward a more distinct position on economic and role-of-government questions. It is certainly possible, given figure 5.1, that the growing polarization of the mass party coalitions on social welfare issues from the mid-1970s to the early 1990s occurred in response to a growing distinctiveness in the social welfare positions of party leaders and party platforms.[4]

Figure 5.2 shows the mean positions of Democratic and Republican identifiers on racial issues from 1956 to 1992. The patterns shown in this figure are very similar to those uncovered by some of our own previous work.[5] Although there was little difference between the party coalitions on racial matters before 1964, Democratic identifiers were slightly more conservative than were Republican identifiers. The 1960–64 period, however, appears to represent a "critical moment" in the partisan alignment on racial issues. Not only is the relationship reversed, with the Republican coalition becoming more racially conservative than the Democratic coalition, but the parties also become much more sharply divided over this period. Following 1964, there is a gradual increase in partisan polarization on the racial dimension.

What is particularly interesting is that while this earlier work documents the growing racial division of the parties, that work ends at the point where a sharp increase in racial polarization begins. After 1984, the rate of partisan change on the racial dimension moves from gradual to rapid, as the Republican coalition becomes notably more conservative and the Democratic coalition becomes distinctly more liberal. It is possible, and in fact likely, that the acceleration of partisan change on racial issues reflects a change in the racial policy agenda, from governmental action to ensure equal opportunity for blacks to affirmative action policies designed to ensure equality of outcomes. While this change occurred before the late 1980s, it was not evident in the presidential year surveys until 1988, when the NES

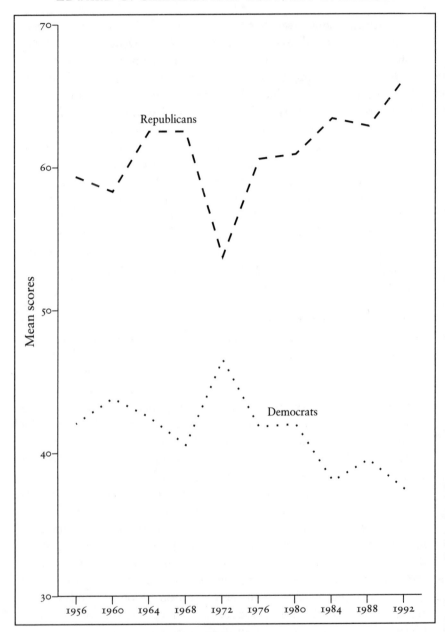

FIGURE 5.1
SOCIAL WELFARE ATTITUDES OF DEMOCRATS
AND REPUBLICANS, 1956–92

SOURCE: American National Election Studies, 1956–92.

NOTE: Higher scores represent more conservative positions.

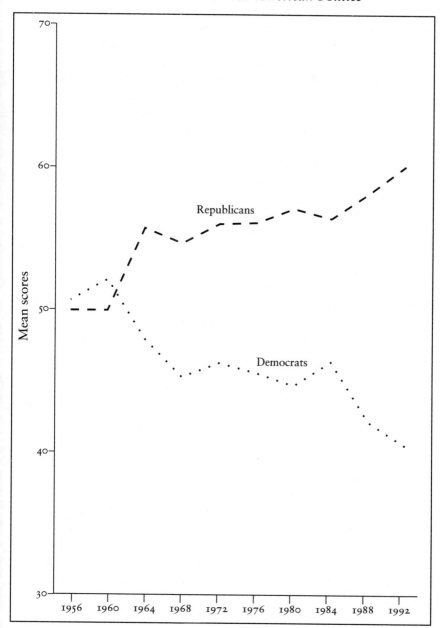

FIGURE 5.2

RACIAL ATTITUDES OF DEMOCRATS AND REPUBLICANS,
1956–92

SOURCE: American National Election Studies, 1956–92.

NOTE: Higher scores represent more conservative positions.

included questions regarding university admission quotas for black students and preference being given to minorities in hiring.

This sharp increase in racial polarization over the 1984–92 period may well be caused by the fact that these highly divisive affirmative action issues are included in the racial issue scale in 1988 and 1992. It is certainly possible that the parties are now more divided on these issues than on the traditional civil rights issues involving equality of opportunity. In fact, affirmative action may not only be creating a greater partisan polarization on racial issues, it also may be leading to further partisan polarization on the basis of race. Given the strong distaste of whites for affirmative action, the Democratic Party's association with these programs may be encouraging an increasing number of whites to leave the party, thus making blacks a bigger part of the Democratic coalition.

Figure 5.3 shows the mean attitudes of Democratic and Republican identifiers on social and cultural issues from 1972 to 1992. Although the growth is not steady, the figure shows a pattern of growing partisan polarization on cultural concerns. There was little or no difference between party coalitions on issues such as abortion and women's rights in the 1970s. But with the arrival of Ronald Reagan as the Republican Party's standard-bearer in 1980 and the entry of the Christian Right into Republican politics in the late 1970s, the parties became much more divided on cultural issues in 1980.[6] Cultural polarization was still quite evident in 1984, but, somewhat surprisingly, the parties became much less distinct on cultural matters in 1988. Between 1988 and 1992, however, there was a sharp increase in the cultural division of the parties' mass coalitions.

Clearly, the postwar period has been one of significant transformation in American party politics. The party coalitions have become increasingly divided on two new issue dimensions: racial and cultural. Moreover, the social welfare cleavage that has traditionally divided Democrats and Republicans appears to have been revitalized as partisan polarization on this dimension gradually increased after the mid-1970s.

Change and Continuity in the Social-Group Bases of Party Support

Changes in the political agenda and in the issue-based cleavages that divide the parties generally are associated with changes in the social-

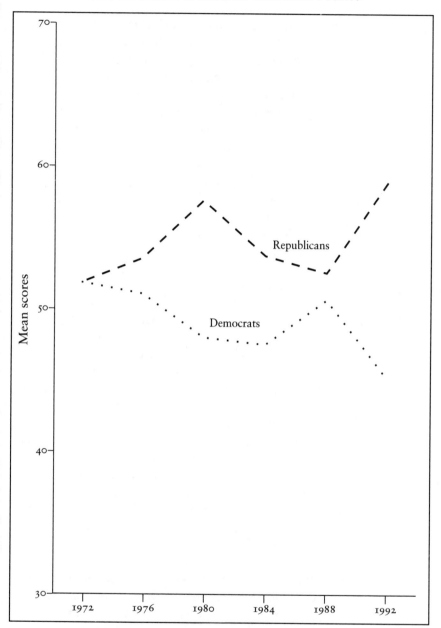

FIGURE 5.3

SOCIAL AND CULTURAL ATTITUDES OF DEMOCRATS
AND REPUBLICANS, 1972–92

SOURCE: American National Election Studies, 1972–92.

NOTE: Higher scores represent more conservative positions.

group composition of the party coalitions.[7] Thus the movement of racial issues and social and cultural issues to the fore of the American political agenda and the increasing polarization of the parties on these issues should be associated with significant changes in the group bases of party support. On the other hand, the introduction of new issues into American party politics does not appear to have resulted in the disappearance of the cleavage that had divided the parties since the 1930s: the social welfare cleavage. The fact that the parties are still quite polarized on social welfare issues and have become increasingly divided on these issues over the past two decades points to the possibility that there has also been a good deal of continuity in the composition of the party coalitions. Since the social welfare cleavage is still quite sharp, many of the groups included in the Democratic and Republican coalitions during the New Deal era may still provide the parties with significant support.

While many groups were included in the Democratic Party's New Deal coalition, the backbone of this coalition was formed by four: poor and working-class citizens, blacks, southerners, and ethnic and religious minorities.[8] In order to examine changes in the strength of this core of the Democratic coalition, we trace the partisanship of lower-income citizens (the bottom third, in terms of percentiles, of the NES income scale), southern whites, blacks, and Catholics over time. Figure 5.4 shows the percentage of each of these four groups identifying with the Democratic Party from 1956 to 1992.

The figure shows that the Democratic Party's association with the agenda of the civil rights movement has indeed been accompanied by the overwhelming support of African Americans for the party. As the parties became associated with more distinct positions on racial issues in the mid-1960s, blacks moved from being solidly Democratic to being overwhelmingly Democratic. While there has been some decline in African American support for the Democrats since the late 1960s, blacks have remained very strongly Democratic.

In the 1950s and early 1960s, the support of southern whites, lower-income citizens, and Catholics for the Democratic Party was as strong as that of African Americans. As blacks have become much more Democratic, however, the party's support from these other groups has declined steadily. As figure 5.4 shows, the patterns for southern whites, lower-income citizens, and Catholics are almost identical. Approximately 60 percent of each of these groups identified with the Democrats in the 1950s and early 1960s. By 1992, only 35 to 40 percent of each group identified themselves as Democrats.

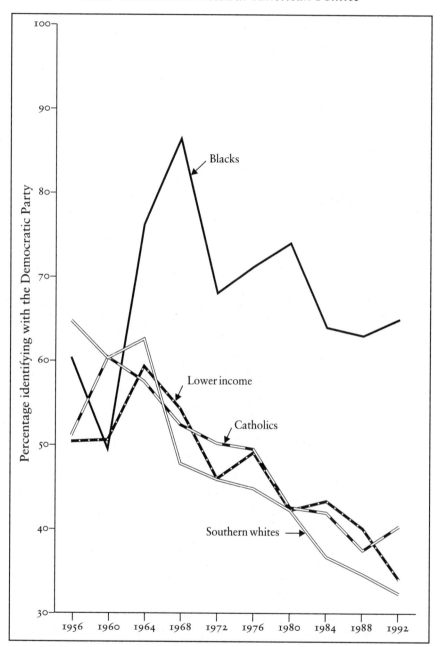

FIGURE 5.4
PERCENTAGE OF TRADITIONALLY DEMOCRATIC GROUPS
IDENTIFYING WITH THE DEMOCRATIC PARTY, 1956–92

SOURCE: American National Election Studies, 1956–92.

Certainly, this decline in Democratic support reflects a general dealignment of party affiliation in the United States: party ties of most social groups have weakened.[9] But it also reflects the emergence of new issues in American politics. The support of lower-income citizens, Catholics, and southern whites for Democratic Party positions on these issues may be less than their support for the party's social welfare stances. It is also possible that, over time, there has been a growing distaste for social welfare liberalism among these groups. Whatever the reason for the weakening of the Democratic core, this deterioration represents a probable explanation for the party's recent electoral troubles: its consistent failures in presidential elections and its loss of control in congressional, state, and local elections.

Since the Republican Party was a distinct minority during the New Deal era, its coalition contained fewer groups than the Democratic coalition. By and large, the Republican coalition was the opposite of the Democratic coalition, but the core of GOP support came from two groups: upper-status citizens and white Protestants living outside the South.[10] But, as a number of scholars have noted, the Republican coalition has grown since the 1950s. Over this period, southern whites have become increasingly Republican. In the late 1970s and early 1980s, evangelical and fundamentalist Christians became increasingly involved in Republican politics, and they have come to represent an increasingly important part of the Republican coalition.[11]

Figure 5.5 shows the percentage of upper-income citizens (the top third, in terms of percentiles, of the NES income scale), white Protestants residing outside the South, southern whites, and religious conservatives (regular attenders of conservative Protestant denominations) identifying with the Republican Party from 1956 to 1992. A comparison of this figure with figure 5.4 provides a good explanation for the Republican Party's growing electoral success over the past three decades. While the Democratic Party has suffered significant losses in support from many of the groups that formed the backbone of its coalition, the groups that formed the core of the Republican coalition have remained solidly Republican.

The percentage of upper-income citizens and of northern white Protestants identifying with the GOP has not declined notably since the 1950s. Meanwhile, the Republican Party has made significant gains among two other groups: southern whites and religious conservatives. The percentage of religious conservatives identifying with the Republican Party was relatively high in 1960, presumably the result of the Democratic Party's nomination of a Catholic presidential candi-

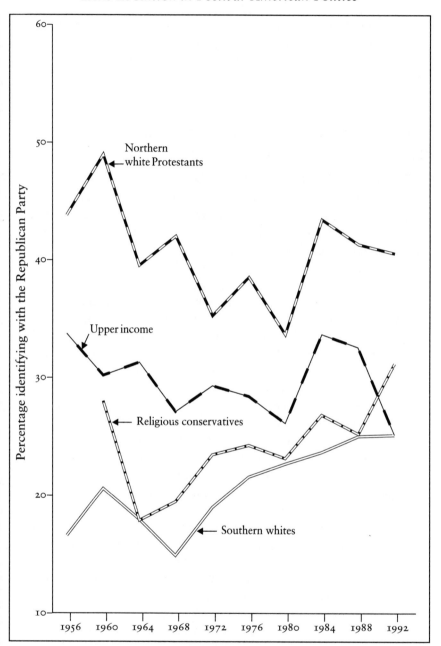

FIGURE 5.5
PERCENTAGE OF VARIOUS GROUPS IDENTIFYING
WITH THE REPUBLICAN PARTY, 1956–92

SOURCE: American National Election Studies, 1956–92.

date. Republican support among religious conservatives dropped sharply in 1964, but rose steadily after 1964. There was a steady increase in the percentage of southern whites identifying with the GOP from 1968 to 1992.

The Link between Issue-Oriented and Group-Oriented Partisan Change: The Issue-Attitudes of Various Social Groups

Much of the group-based partisan change that has occurred since 1956 is likely to be related to the emergence of new issue-based cleavages in American politics. These new cleavages tend to crosscut the social welfare cleavage that traditionally has structured American party coalitions so that groups that tended to support one party's positions on the social welfare dimension tend to support the other party's positions on the new dimensions. For instance, the emergence of social and cultural issues on the political scene may be associated with a reversal of the class basis of partisan support. Lower-income voters, who have traditionally supported the Democratic Party's liberal social welfare positions, tend to take conservative stances on cultural matters. Upper-income voters, who have traditionally supported the Republican Party's conservative social welfare positions, tend to take liberal stances on social and cultural issues.[12]

The emergence of new issue dimensions may also be associated with the emergence of new groups in the party coalitions. For instance, the movement of cultural issues to the political forefront may have led to the increasing Republicanism of religious conservatives, since religious conservatism is strongly linked with conservative cultural attitudes.[13] In order to examine the link between issue-oriented partisan change and the change in group-based partisan support, we examine the positions of seven groups—upper-income citizens, lower-income citizens, southern whites, blacks, Catholics, religious conservatives, and northern white Protestants—on social welfare, racial, and social and cultural issues over time.

Figure 5.6 shows the mean social welfare attitudes of these seven groups from 1956 to 1992. As the figure makes plain, the group that differs most from other groups on these issues is blacks. Clearly, the strong support of African Americans for the Democratic Party, both before and after partisan polarization on racial issues, in part reflects their staunch liberalism on social welfare matters. Lower-income vot-

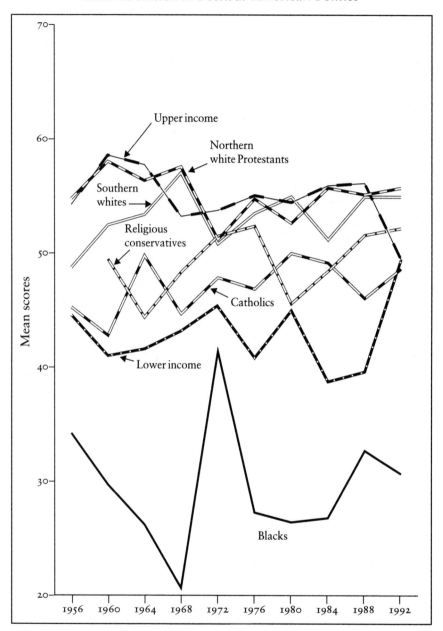

FIGURE 5.6
SOCIAL WELFARE ATTITUDES OF VARIOUS SOCIAL GROUPS,
1956–92

SOURCE: American National Election Studies, 1956–92.

NOTE: Higher scores represent more conservative positions.

ers are also quite liberal on social welfare issues throughout this period. Thus it is unlikely that their declining identification with the Democratic Party is due to the party's liberalism on these matters. Since religious conservatives tend to fluctuate around the mean social welfare attitude for all respondents ($x = 50$), it seems unlikely that their growing Republicanism can be attributed to the party's social welfare positions. It also seems somewhat unlikely that Catholics have become less attached to the Democratic Party because of the party's liberal social welfare stances, since Catholics are slightly below the mean throughout most of this period.

The fact that upper-income citizens and northern white Protestants have fairly conservative social welfare attitudes throughout the period is quite consistent with their relatively unchanging support for the Republican Party. It appears that the party's opposition to welfare liberalism appeals as much to these groups now as it ever has. It is, however, interesting that the drop shown in figure 5.5 in the Republicanism of upper-income citizens from 1988 to 1992 is accompanied by a fairly sharp drop in the social welfare conservatism of this group. While this cannot yet be called a trend, it may be that the sample of upper-income respondents in the 1992 NES was less conservative on social welfare matters than in previous years, and this may account for their weaker attachments to the GOP. While the movement of southern whites out of the Democratic Party and into the Republican Party generally has been attributed to their conservatism on racial matters, it may also be the result of their distaste for the Democrats' (liberal) social welfare positions.[14] White southerners became consistently more conservative on these matters from 1956 to 1968, and have remained relatively conservative since then.

Figure 5.7 shows the mean racial attitudes of the seven social groups from 1956 to 1992. As the figure shows, two groups are clearly distinguished from the rest by their racial attitudes. Blacks have considerably more liberal positions on racial issues, while southern whites are notably more racially conservative than the rest of these groups. It is clear that the growth in black support for the Democratic Party in the 1960s and their consistently solid Democratic ties since then have been in large part a result of the parties' liberal stands on racial matters. It is also clear that the exodus of southern whites from the Democratic Party is attributable in large part to the party's racial liberalism. Most of the other groups have mean racial attitudes that fluctuate closely around the population mean. It is thus unlikely that much of the change or continuity in their patterns of partisan support

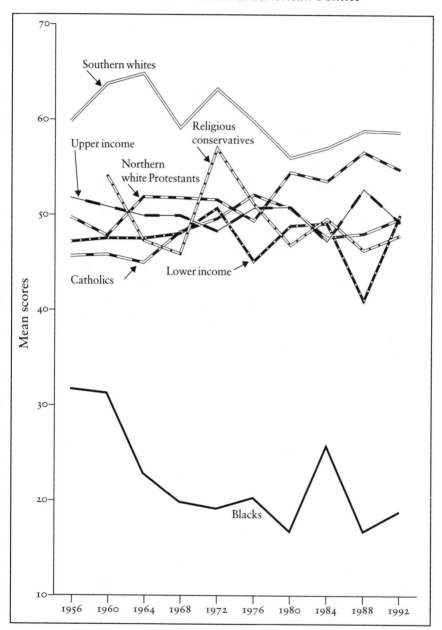

FIGURE 5.7
RACIAL ATTITUDES OF VARIOUS SOCIAL GROUPS,
1956–92

SOURCE: American National Election Studies, 1956–92.

NOTE: Higher scores represent more conservative positions.

reflects partisan polarization on racial issues. The one exception to this may be white Protestants residing outside the South, since they have relatively conservative racial attitudes throughout most of the period. Part of the reason for the consistently strong Republicanism of this group may be its continuing opposition to racial liberalism.

Figure 5.8 shows the mean attitudes of these seven groups on social and cultural issues from 1972 to 1992. Three of the groups—blacks, Catholics, and northern white Protestants—have cultural attitudes that tend to fluctuate about the population mean. Northern white Protestants are slightly more conservative than the average NES respondent, so their consistent support for the GOP may be partly attributable to the party's conservative cultural stances. Blacks tend to have relatively moderate cultural positions, with the exception of their very conservative positions in 1984. Their overwhelming support for the Democratic Party appears to reflect the party's liberalism on racial and social welfare issues and not the party's liberal cultural stances. While many pundits have argued that the conservatism of Catholics on issues such as abortion has driven them out of the Democratic coalition, they do not appear to be consistently conservative on the overall complex of social and cultural issues.

Given the large number of groups included in figure 5.8, it may be somewhat difficult to detect the fact that four groups—religious conservatives, lower-income citizens, southern whites, and upper-income citizens—have cultural attitudes that consistently are either above or below the population mean. Figure 5.9 shows the mean cultural attitudes of these four groups, excluding the three groups in figure 5.8 whose positions tend to fluctuate around the population mean. Figure 5.9 thus provides a clear explanation of the increasing Republicanism of religious conservatives. This group has cultural attitudes that are very conservative and are consistently more conservative than the other social groups. Clearly, religious conservatives have been attracted into the GOP by the party's growing conservatism on cultural matters. It is also clear that the Republican Party's cultural conservatism has reinforced the appeal its racial conservatism holds for southern whites. White southerners have consistently conservative cultural positions.

Figure 5.9 also points to the possibility of a reversal of the class basis of partisanship as cultural issues become more important in American politics. Lower-income citizens have consistently conservative cultural attitudes, while upper-income citizens have consistently liberal positions on these matters. Partisan polarization on cultural is-

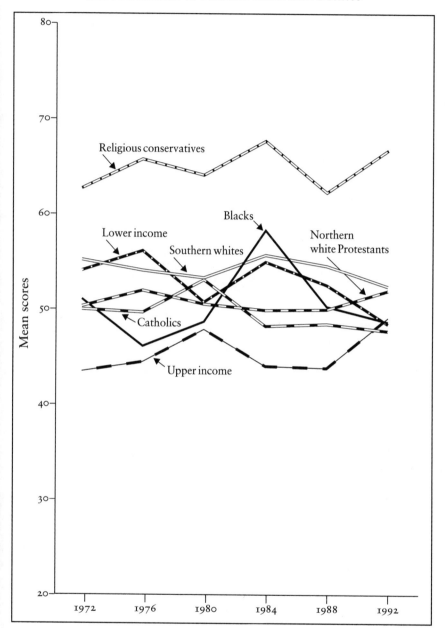

FIGURE 5.8
SOCIAL AND CULTURAL ATTITUDES OF VARIOUS
SOCIAL GROUPS, 1972–92

SOURCE: American National Election Studies, 1972–92.

NOTE: Higher scores represent more conservative positions.

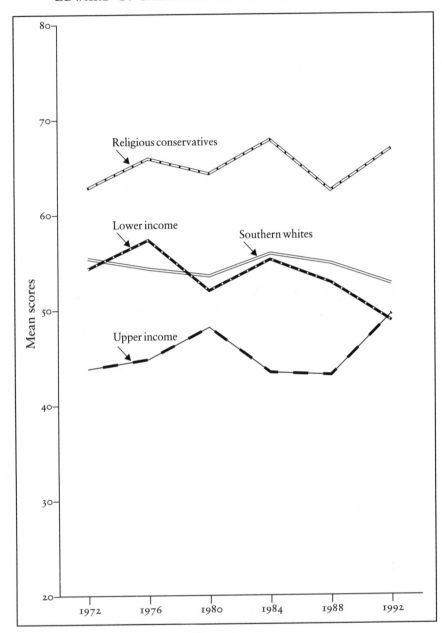

FIGURE 5.9

SOCIAL AND CULTURAL ATTITUDES OF FOUR SOCIAL GROUPS,
1972–92

SOURCE: American National Election Studies, 1972–92.

NOTE: Higher scores represent more conservative positions.

sues may be part of the reason for the partial abandonment of the Democratic Party by lower-income citizens. While upper-income citizens have not shown many signs of deserting the Republican Party, the further movement of cultural issues to the forefront of American politics and the further polarization of the parties on these issues may lead them to rethink and perhaps reshape their partisan ties.

Intraparty Conflict on Various Issue Dimensions

From the perspective of the issue attitudes of entire groups, there certainly appears to be a good deal of disagreement within the party coalitions on various domestic political issues. On social welfare and racial issues, there are substantial disparities in the positions of two traditionally Democratic groups: African Americans and southern whites. On social and cultural issues, there is substantial tension within the Republican Party: the positions of upper-income citizens, who have traditionally constituted the core of the Republican coalition, stand in stark contrast to those of religious conservatives, who have come to represent an increasing proportion of that coalition.

Despite these disagreements between groups from which the two parties hope to draw support, there may be considerably less conflict within what might more accurately be termed the party coalitions: among those citizens who actually identify themselves with the party. It is possible that as the parties have become increasingly polarized on each of these three issue dimensions, they have begun to appeal only to certain portions of the groups from which they have traditionally derived support.[15] For instance, as the Democratic Party becomes more liberal on social welfare, racial, and cultural matters, those southern whites, lower-income citizens, and Catholics who continue to support it would be those with more liberal stances on these issues. Similarly, as the Republican Party becomes more conservative on these issues, those upper-income citizens and northern Protestants who continue to identify themselves as Republicans would be those with more conservative cultural, racial, and social welfare stances.

If true, this scenario has both favorable and unfavorable ramifications for the parties. On the positive side, the parties would find it easier to maintain the support of their electoral coalitions under this scenario than they would if their supporters from various groups were as ideologically diverse as are the groups themselves. On the negative side, ideological homogeneity among party identifiers may indicate that the party has alienated those members of traditionally supportive groups who disagree with the dominant view within the party. For instance, white southern Democrats may be considerably more liberal on matters of race now than they were in the 1960s, but the proportion of southern whites also may have dwindled to the point that only the racially liberal among them still identify with the Democratic Party. This section addresses the question of intraparty conflict by examining the attitudes on various issue dimensions of those members of traditionally supportive groups who identify themselves with the party.

Before examining the degree of intraparty division on social welfare issues, it first should be noted that throughout this period there have been large partisan differences on social welfare issues within groups. Within most social groups, Republican identifiers have been substantially more conservative than Democratic identifiers.[16] It does appear that the polarization of the parties along the lines of social welfare issues has led them not only to be more attractive to different groups but also to attract different portions of the same groups—those portions in agreement with the dominant views in the party.

In the case of the Democrats, however, the fact that there are substantial partisan differences within groups on social welfare matters does not mean that there is little ideological conflict among party identifiers. Figure 5.10 shows the mean attitudes on social welfare issues from 1956 to 1992 of Democratic identifiers within four groups that have traditionally supported the Democratic Party: lower-income citizens, southern whites, African Americans, and Catholics. While Democratic identifiers within all four of these groups have generally been more liberal than the average NES respondent ($x = 50$), there has still been a good deal of intraparty tension on social welfare. The greatest conflict among Democrats is, not surprisingly, between white Democrats in the South, whose welfare attitudes fluctuate about the population mean, and lower-income citizens and African Americans, who tend to have quite liberal attitudes on matters of social welfare. The difficulties the national Democratic Party has faced in attempting to maintain a coalition of southern whites and lower-status and minority voters are clearly evident in this figure.

Figure 5.11 shows the mean social welfare attitudes from 1956 to 1992 of Republican identifiers within two groups—upper-income citizens and northern white Protestants—that have traditionally supported the GOP and within two groups—southern whites and religious conservatives—that have come to represent an increasing presence within the Republican coalition in recent years. The fact that the

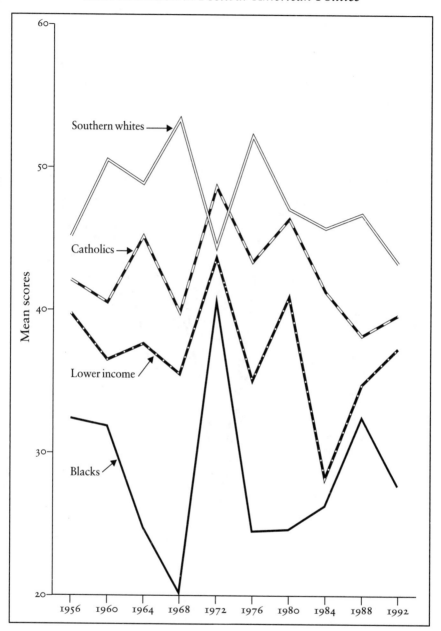

FIGURE 5.10

SOCIAL WELFARE ATTITUDES OF DEMOCRATIC IDENTIFIERS
IN VARIOUS SOCIAL GROUPS, 1956–92

SOURCE: American National Election Studies, 1956–92.

NOTE: Higher scores represent more conservative positions.

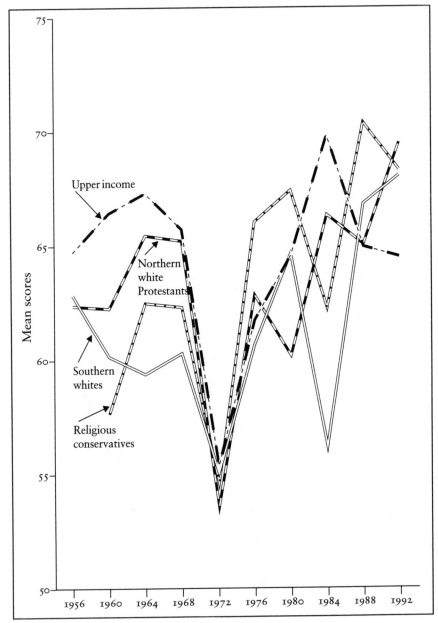

FIGURE 5.11

SOCIAL WELFARE ATTITUDES OF REPUBLICAN IDENTIFIERS
IN VARIOUS SOCIAL GROUPS, 1956–92

SOURCE: American National Election Studies, 1956–92.

NOTE: Higher scores represent more conservative positions.

lines representing each of these groups are jumbled to a large extent indicates that there has been little conflict within the Republican coalition over social welfare issues. Republican identifiers within each of these groups have been quite conservative with regard to social welfare throughout this time period.

The pattern of partisan division within groups on racial issues follows closely the temporal pattern in the nature of the party positions on civil rights matters. Prior to 1964, the party elites were virtually indistinguishable on matters of race. This is evident in the fact that there was little difference between Republican and Democratic identifiers within groups on racial issues in 1956 and 1960. Beginning in 1964, the party elites became increasingly polarized on racial issues. This is apparent in the relatively large partisan differences on racial matters that have existed since 1964. The one exception to this can be found among southern whites. Prior to 1988, partisan differences within this group were quite small, as both white southern Democrats and white southern Republicans were quite conservative on racial issues. Only since 1988 have substantial partisan differences emerged among southern whites on racial issues.[17]

As is the case with social welfare issues, partisan divisions within groups are not associated with internal harmony on racial issues for the Democratic Party. Figure 5.12 shows the mean racial attitudes from 1956 through 1992 of Democratic identifiers within the traditionally Democratic groups; the pattern is one of substantial intraparty conflict. Lower-income and Catholic Democrats have taken very moderate positions on racial issues, southern white Democrats have had conservative positions, and black Democrats have had very liberal racial attitudes. The problems the Democratic Party faces in attempting to maintain its coalition are made even more clear in this figure than in figure 5.10. Given the staunch opposition of southern whites to liberal racial policies, the possibilities of the Democratic Party's responding to the civil rights demands of its black constituents and still maintaining the undivided support of white Democratic identifiers in the South seem to be quite slim.

Figure 5.13 plots the mean racial attitude scores from 1956 through 1992 of Republican identifiers among upper-income citizens, southern whites, northern white Protestants, and religious conservatives. Racial issues are considerably less disruptive for the Republican Party than they are for the Democratic Party (figure 5.12). Southern whites are clearly the most conservative Republicans on matters of race. Nevertheless, their increasing presence in the party does not

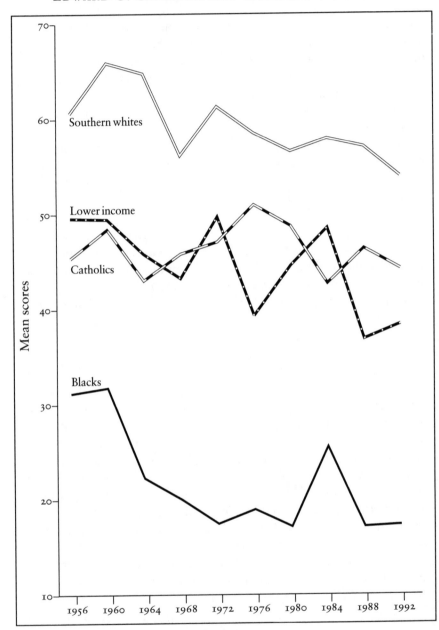

FIGURE 5.12

RACIAL ATTITUDES OF DEMOCRATIC IDENTIFIERS
IN VARIOUS SOCIAL GROUPS, 1956–92

SOURCE: American National Election Studies, 1956–92.

NOTE: Higher scores represent more conservative positions.

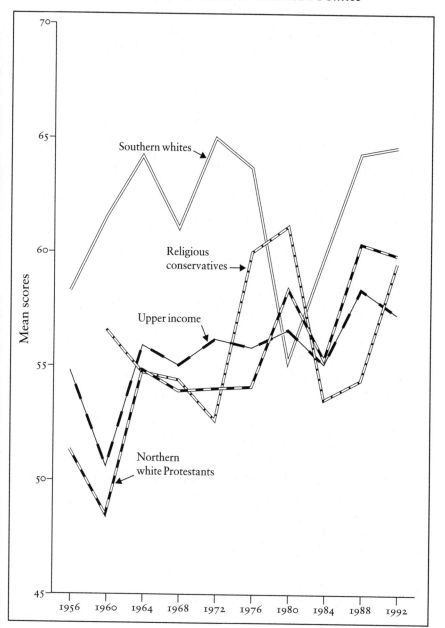

FIGURE 5.13

RACIAL ATTITUDES OF REPUBLICAN IDENTIFIERS
IN VARIOUS SOCIAL GROUPS, 1956–92

SOURCE: American National Election Studies, 1956–92.

NOTE: Higher scores represent more conservative positions.

seem to point to major intraparty conflict on racial issues, as Republican identifiers within the other groups have taken increasingly conservative racial stands as well.

The partisan differences within groups on social and cultural issues are not as great as they are on social welfare and racial issues. This discrepancy may change, however, as the parties and their elites become increasingly polarized on cultural matters. Partisan differences since 1980 have been notably larger than partisan differences before 1980, a change that coincides with the growing cultural division of Democratic and Republican elites.[18] The one exception to this is found again among southern whites, where there was little partisan difference until 1988 and especially 1992.[19]

Figure 5.14 shows the mean social and cultural attitudes of Democratic identifiers within traditionally Democratic groups from 1972 to 1992. The figure seems to indicate that there is less internal division within the Democratic coalition on these issues than there is on social welfare and racial issues. In general, it is very difficult to distinguish between the cultural attitudes of lower-income Democrats, white southern Democrats, black Democrats, and Catholic Democrats. While the relative homogeneity of its coalition on these issues may be good news for the Democratic Party, the bad news is that these groups of identifiers are not uniformly liberal. Instead, their attitudes on social and cultural issues range from slightly liberal to slightly conservative.

This could pose a problem for the national Democratic Party, since it has clearly sided with groups such as homosexuals, feminists, and abortion rights activists on cultural matters. Over the past two decades, Democratic activists and Democratic Party platforms have taken increasingly liberal stands on issues such as abortion rights, women's roles, and homosexual discrimination.[20] If this cultural liberalism is not muted, the party's cultural positions will be increasingly out of step with those of many of the groups that have traditionally supported Democratic candidates.

Figure 5.15 shows the mean social and cultural attitudes from 1972 to 1992 of Republican identifiers among upper-income citizens, southern whites, northern white Protestants, and religious conservatives. As the figure makes plain, cultural issues play a more divisive role within the Republican coalition than do racial and social welfare issues. While Republican identifiers among southern whites and northern white Protestants have relatively conservative cultural attitudes and upper-income Republicans have fairly moderate cultural

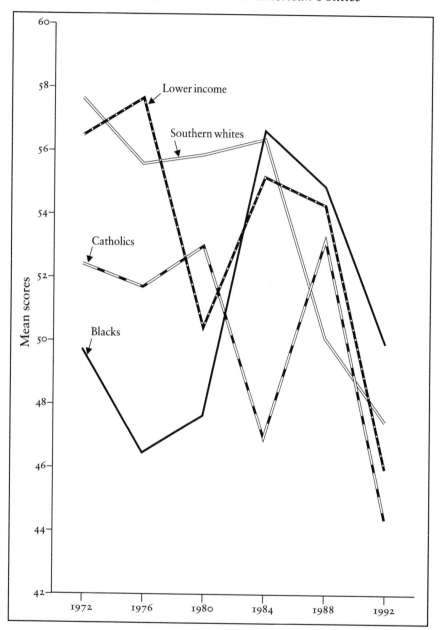

FIGURE 5.14
SOCIAL AND CULTURAL ATTITUDES OF DEMOCRATIC
IDENTIFIERS IN VARIOUS SOCIAL GROUPS, 1972–92

SOURCE: American National Election Studies, 1972–92.

NOTE: Higher scores represent more conservative positions.

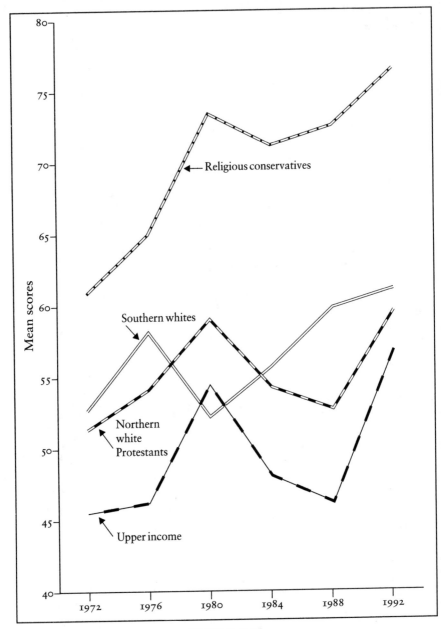

FIGURE 5.15

SOCIAL AND CULTURAL ATTITUDES OF REPUBLICAN
IDENTIFIERS IN VARIOUS SOCIAL GROUPS, 1972–92

SOURCE: American National Election Studies, 1972–92.

NOTE: Higher scores represent more conservative positions.

positions, Republican religious conservatives are extremely conservative when it comes to cultural matters.

The cultural conservatism expressed in recent Republican platforms certainly appeals to the evangelical and fundamentalist Christians who have become increasingly involved in the party over the past two decades, and should help the GOP to make further gains among religious conservatives. But at the same time, extreme conservatism on cultural matters also has the potential to alienate those groups who have typically supported the Republican Party, particularly upper-status voters who traditionally have constituted the core of Republican electoral coalitions. Just as racial issues have been dangerous for the Democratic Party, the newer social and cultural issues appear to be dangerous for the Republican Party. While they may attract groups that previously have not supported the party, they may also lead traditionally Republican groups to defect.

Conclusion

Statistical evidence on issue conflict in postwar American politics points to three major conclusions. The first is that the parties now differ from one another across the full domestic policy spectrum. Historically, the parties took distinct stands on social welfare and role-of-government issues. But the two new issue dimensions emerging in the postwar era, focusing on race and culture, also have become partisan issues. Thus Republicans and Democrats now consistently oppose each other on domestic policy issues; the former is a full-fledged conservative party, the latter an increasingly liberal party. It should not be surprising, then, that liberal (or even moderate) Republicans and conservative Democrats have become endangered species in contemporary American politics.

The second major conclusion concerns the changes in relative support for the postwar Democratic and Republican parties. While blacks have become a larger part of the Democratic coalition, the party has suffered significant losses within its white New Deal base. Catholics, lower-income earners, and especially white southerners have shown a declining tendency to support the postwar Democratic Party. By contrast, the GOP continues to receive strong support from traditional Republican groups, notably higher-income earners and northern white Protestants. In addition, both southern whites and religious conservatives have become more Republican over the last three decades.

These changes in the social-group basis of the post–New Deal party system are clearly linked to political issues, especially the new issues of race and culture. Southern whites are consistently conservative and, as a result, have found themselves opposed to the Democratic Party's liberalism not just on race but also on social welfare and social and cultural issues. Thus it is not surprising that they have moved strongly toward the GOP. Similarly, the undiluted liberalism of blacks on both social welfare and racial issues no doubt accounts for their growing support for the Democratic Party. And clearly the extremely conservative social and cultural attitudes of religious conservatives have been the main factor in moving them toward the GOP.

Finally, this research sheds light on intraparty conflict in postwar American politics. Social welfare issues are not very divisive within each party coalition. Republicans, in particular, are largely unified on social welfare issues; all of their constituent social groups have markedly conservative positions on social welfare. It is true that black and lower-income Democrats have more liberal positions on social welfare issues than do white southern Democrats. But all of the Democratic core groups, including the southern wing, are on the liberal side of this ideological divide.

Racial issues, however, continue to divide the contemporary Democratic Party. Southern white Democrats are modestly conservative on racial issues, while blacks are extremely liberal. Given this discrepancy, it may prove very difficult for the Democratic Party in the South to maintain a viable biracial electoral coalition. Conversely, Republicans are well-positioned to exploit this opportunity, since they have uniformly conservative racial views, which are quite attractive to southern white Democrats. Thus racial issues continue to divide the core Democratic Party, a division that Republicans have repeatedly taken advantage of in postwar America.

If racial issues have proved to be disruptive to the post–New Deal Democratic Party, social and cultural issues have this potential for the GOP. These issues pit upper-income Republicans, who have fairly moderate views on social and cultural concerns, against Republican religious conservatives, who are extremely conservative on cultural matters. So far, the GOP has been fairly successful in holding on to its core groups, but if the party continues to move toward the cultural right, it may have real difficulty retaining its traditional base. Drawn to the GOP because of its conservative economic and social welfare stands, well-to-do Republicans may desert the party because of its extreme cultural conservatism.

The simple equilibrium that existed in American politics when the parties mainly fought over New Deal social welfare issues is gone. But no new equilibrium has yet replaced it. Instead, the newer issues of race and culture have led to major divisions within the parties as well as polarization between them. These issues have transformed the New Deal party system," but no new stable alignment has yet emerged. We have been reduced to speaking of a "post–New Deal party system," which may be the inevitable result of party competition in a multidimensional issue world.

Appendix A
Factor Analysis of Issue Indicators

This appendix presents the results of factor analyses, using principal-components extraction and varimax rotation, of the indicators of domestic policy attitudes included in the 1956–92 National Election Studies. All tables follow the same format. Table A.1, for example, presents the results of the factor analysis for 1956. Two factors emerge from the analysis, with social welfare attitudes loading strongly on one factor and civil rights attitudes loading strongly on another. The first factor has an eigenvalue of 1.6 and explains 39.78 percent of the total variance; the second factor has an eigenvalue of 1.0 and explains 24.8 percent of the variance. Tables A.2 (for 1960) through A.4 (for 1968) produce highly parallel results.

With table A.5, the results of the factor analysis for 1972, the analysis begins to uncover three factors, with racial attitudes loading strongly on the first, attitudes on social and cultural issues loading strongly on the second, and economic and social welfare attitudes loading strongly on the third. The first factor then has an eigenvalue of 2.0 and explains 27 percent of the total variance; the second factor has an eigenvalue of 1.2 and explains 10.3 percent of the variance; the third factor has an eigenvalue of 1.1 and explains 8.6 percent of the total variance. Tables A.6 (from 1976) through A.10 (for 1992) again produce highly parallel results.

TABLE A.1

RESULTS OF FACTOR ANALYSIS OF ISSUE ATTITUDES,

1956

Issues	Factor 1	Factor 2
Social welfare		
Government role in providing housing and utilities	.814	−.094
Government role in providing medical services	.741	.156
Racial		
Black housing and employment	.241	.784
School integration	.086	.810
Eigenvalues	1.6	1.0
Variance explained	39.7	24.8

SOURCE: American National Election Study for the relevant year. Issue scales are formed by summing the individual items on the corresponding factor. All issues range from the most liberal to the most conservative positions.

TABLE A.2

RESULTS OF FACTOR ANALYSIS OF ISSUE ATTITUDES,

1960

Issues	Factor 1	Factor 2
Racial		
School integration	.857	.137
Black housing and employment	.816	.086
Social welfare		
Government guarantee of jobs	.263	.768
Government aid to education	.275	.740
Government provision of medical services	.220	.751
Eigenvalues	2.2	1.1
Variance explained	36.6	19.2

TABLE A.3
RESULTS OF FACTOR ANALYSIS OF ISSUE ATTITUDES,
1964

Issues	Factor 1	Factor 2
Social welfare		
Government provision of medical services	.788	−.029
Government guarantee of jobs	.824	−.032
Racial		
Fair employment practices	.525	.572
Pace of the civil rights movement	.344	.632
Housing integration	.047	.779
School integration	.287	.744
Eigenvalues	2.5	1.2
Variance explained	41.3	19.8

TABLE A.4
RESULTS OF FACTOR ANALYSIS OF ISSUE ATTITUDES,
1968

Issues	Factor 1	Factor 2
Racial		
Pace of the civil rights movement	.772	.206
Urban unrest	.818	.141
Social welfare		
Government provision of medical services	−.037	.829
Government guarantee of jobs	.252	.724
Government aid to education	.252	.686
Eigenvalues	2.2	1.0
Variance explained	43.9	18.9

TABLE A.5

RESULTS OF FACTOR ANALYSIS OF ISSUE ATTITUDES,

1972

Issues	Factor 1	Factor 2	Factor 3
Racial			
Urban unrest	.591	.158	.082
Rights of the accused	.552	.200	−.002
Government help for blacks	.705	.172	.084
Pace of the civil rights movement	.641	.187	−.041
Amount of black influence	.700	−.036	−.107
Fairness in jobs	.567	−.141	.201
Busing to integrate schools	.586	.196	.125
Social and cultural			
Abortion	.018	.766	.050
Women's role in society	.126	.573	.057
Legalization of marijuana	.372	.598	−.048
Economic and social welfare			
Government action against inflation	.079	−.248	.640
Changes in tax rates	−.004	.191	.757
Eigenvalues	2.0	1.2	1.1
Variance explained	27.0	10.3	8.6

TABLE A.6
RESULTS OF FACTOR ANALYSIS OF ISSUE ATTITUDES,
1976

Issues	Factor 1	Factor 2	Factor 3
Racial			
School desegregation	.693	.125	−.055
Pace of the civil rights movement	.688	.130	.152
Busing to integrate schools	.651	.033	.172
Urban unrest	.501	.144	.316
Rights of the accused	.478	.187	.068
Government help for blacks	.595	.071	.438
Social and cultural			
Abortion	−.019	.801	−.042
Legalization of marijuana	.197	.718	.128
Women's role in society	.209	.618	.111
Economic and social welfare			
Government guarantee of jobs	.243	−.067	.696
Government provision of health insurance	.076	.153	.749
Changes in tax rates	−.050	.008	.500
Eigenvalues	3.3	1.4	1.0
Variance explained	27.3	11.5	8.6

TABLE A.7

RESULTS OF FACTOR ANALYSIS OF ISSUE ATTITUDES,
1980

Issues	Factor 1	Factor 2	Factor 3
Racial			
Busing to integrate schools	.067	.008	.851
Pace of the civil rights movement	.183	.126	.741
Social and cultural			
Women's role in society	.065	.756	.082
Abortion	−.084	.734	−.115
School prayer	−.131	.572	.240
Equal rights amendment	.304	.594	.252
Economic and social welfare			
Government services and spending	.804	.124	.126
Government attention to inflation vs.	.746	−.158	−.022
Unemployment	.654	.065	.326
Eigenvalues	2.5	1.7	1.0
Variance explained	27.3	18.8	11.4

TABLE A.8

RESULTS OF FACTOR ANALYSIS OF ISSUE ATTITUDES,

1984

Issues	Factor 1	Factor 2	Factor 3
Racial			
Busing to integrate schools	.202	.008	.671
Pace of the civil rights movement	.126	.140	.744
Change in the position of blacks	−.099	−.022	.572
Social and cultural			
Abortion	.032	.771	−.059
Women's role in society	.157	.624	.157
School prayer	−.032	.651	.177
Economic and social welfare			
Spending on Social Security	.694	−.044	−.034
Government services and spending	.674	.065	.183
Spending on food stamp programs	.622	.176	.277
Government guarantee of jobs	.680	.044	.175
Government provision of health insurance	.629	.033	−.091
Eigenvalues	2.7	1.4	1.1
Variance explained	24.5	13.2	10.4

TABLE A.9

RESULTS OF FACTOR ANALYSIS OF ISSUE ATTITUDES,

1988

Issues	Factor 1	Factor 2	Factor 3
Racial			
Black student quotas	.799	−.079	.093
Preferential hiring of blacks	.746	−.072	.125
Government help for blacks	.594	.048	.365
Spending on programs for blacks	.589	.140	.327
Fair employment practices	.627	.145	.149
Pace of the civil rights movement	.531	.399	.048
Death penalty	.534	.204	.051
Social and cultural			
Women's role in society	.021	.661	−.021
Abortion	−.097	.712	.077
Laws to protect homosexuals against discrimination	.348	.511	.088
School prayer	−.002	.573	.051
Economic and social welfare			
Spending on Social Security	−.171	−.144	.572
Government services and spending	.248	.164	.611
Spending to help the homeless	.387	−.143	.500
Spending to help the unemployed	.306	.048	.611
Government provision of health insurance	.063	.204	.622
Government guarantee of jobs	.295	.001	.551
Spending on food stamp programs	.486	.025	.520
Eigenvalues	5.0	1.8	1.4
Variance explained	27.7	9.8	7.7

TABLE A.IO

RESULTS OF FACTOR ANALYSIS OF ISSUE ATTITUDES,
1992

Issues	Factor 1	Factor 2	Factor 3
Racial			
Black student quotas	.792	.044	.154
Preferential hiring of blacks	.727	.057	.042
Spending on programs for blacks	.704	.084	.250
Government help for blacks	.700	.178	.220
School integration	.593	.104	.179
Pace of the civil rights movement	.536	.204	.197
Fair employment practices	.591	.123	.165
Social and cultural			
Abortion	−.027	.783	.019
Husband's consent for wife to have abortion	.128	.703	−.129
Allowing homosexuals to adopt children	.284	.591	.218
Allowing homosexuals in the military	.170	.602	.284
Laws to protect homosexuals against discrimination	.179	.456	.394
Parental consent for abortion	.237	.586	−.031
Government funding of abortion	.160	.551	.246
Women's role in society	−.088	.577	.078
School prayer	−.035	.401	.050
Economic and social welfare			
Spending to help the poor	.211	.026	.719
Spending to help the unemployed	.231	−.044	.683
Spending to help the homeless	.094	.077	.665
Government services and spending	.174	.138	.624
Government guarantee of jobs	.341	.089	.522
Government provision of health insurance	.110	.189	.520
Welfare spending	.396	.105	.510
Eigenvalues	6.3	2.5	1.6
Variance explained	27.5	10.7	6.9

Appendix B

THE RELIABILITY OF THE ISSUE SCALES

Year	Racial	Social welfare	Social and cultural
1956	.50	.37	—
1960	.57	.71	—
1964	.67	.58	—
1968	.49	.65	—
1972	.75	.20	.55
1976	.72	.43	.60
1980	.52	.66	.61
1984	.40	.71	.52
1988	.82	.74	.52
1992	.82	.76	.74

SOURCE: American National Election Studies, 1956–92. All entries are reliability coefficient alpha.

Notes

1. Byron E. Shafer and William J.M. Claggett, *The Two Majorities: The Issue Substance of Modern American Politics* (Baltimore: Johns Hopkins University Press, 1995).

2. E.J. Dionne Jr., *Why Americans Hate Politics* (New York: Simon and Schuster, 1991), 43.

3. For each year included in the analysis, attitudes toward social welfare, racial, and social and cultural issues are measured by summing respondent scores on those indicators with factor loadings of .4 or above on each particular factor. The resulting indices are then standardized to a mean of 50 and a standard deviation of 25. Higher scores on each dimension represent more conservative positions. The reliability coefficient (alpha) for each of these issue scales is shown in appendix B.

4. Edward G. Carmines and James A. Stimson, *Issue Evolution: Race and the Transformation of American Politics* (Princeton: Princeton University Press, 1989); and James L. Sundquist, *Dynamics of the Party System: Alignment and Realignment of Political Parties in the United States*, rev. ed. (Washington, D.C.: Brookings Institution, 1983).

5. Carmines and Stimson, *Issue Evolution*.

6. James L. Guth, "The New Christian Right," in *The New Christian Right: Religion and Politics in the 1988 Election*, ed. Robert C. Liebman and Robert Wuthnow (Boulder, Colo.: Westview, 1991); James Davison Hunter, *American Evangelicalism: Conservative Religion and the Quandary of Mo-*

dernity (New Brunswick: Rutgers University Press, 1983); and Steve Bruce, *The Rise and Fall of the New Christian Right: Conservative Protestant Politics in America, 1978–1988* (New York: Oxford University Press, 1988).

7. John R. Petrocik, *Party Coalitions and the Decline of the New Deal Party System* (Chicago: University of Chicago Press, 1981); and Sundquist, *Dynamics of the Party System.*

8. Robert Axelrod, "Where the Votes Come From: An Analysis of Electoral Coalitions," *American Political Science Review* 66 (March 1972): 11–20; and Sundquist, *Dynamics of the Party System.*

9. Paul Allen Beck, "The Dealignment Era in America," in *Electoral Change in Advanced Industrial Democracies: Realignment or Dealignment?* ed. Russell J. Dalton, Scott C. Flanagan, and Paul Allen Beck (Princeton: Princeton University Press, 1984); Harold W. Stanley and Richard G. Niemi, "The Demise of the New Deal Coalition: Partisanship and Group Support, 1952–1992," in *Democracy's Feast: Elections in America,* ed. Herbert F. Weisberg (Chatham, N.J.: Chatham House, 1995).

10. Axelrod, "Where the Votes Come From"; and Sundquist, *Dynamics of the Party System.*

11. Guth, "The New Christian Right"; Arthur H. Miller and Martin P. Wattenberg, "Politics from the Pulpit: Religiosity and the 1980 Elections," *Public Opinion Quarterly* 48 (Spring 1984): 301–17; and John C. Green, "The Christian Right and the 1994 Elections: A View from the States," *PS* 28 (March 1995): 5–8.

12. Everett Carll Ladd Jr. with Charles D. Hadley, *Transformations of the American Party System* (New York: Norton, 1975); James Woods, "Tension in the Party System: The Social and Cultural Issue Agenda," Ph.D. dissertation, Indiana University, 1993; and Edward G. Carmines, "Political Issues, Party Alignment, Spatial Models, and the Post–New Deal Party System," in *New Perspectives in American Politics,* ed. Lawrence C. Dodd and Calvin Jillson (Washington, D.C.: CQ Press, 1994).

13. Ted Jelen, *The Political Mobilization of Religious Beliefs* (New York: Praeger, 1991); John C. Green, James L. Guth, and Cleveland R. Fraser, "Apostles and Apostates? Religion and Politics among Party Activities," in *The Bible and the Ballot Box: Religion and Politics in the 1988 Election,* ed. James L. Guth and John C. Green (Boulder, Colo.: Westview, 1991); and Geoffrey C. Layman, "Parties and Culture Wars: The Manifestation of Cultural Conflict in the American Party System," Ph.D. dissertation, Indiana University, 1995.

14. Edward G. Carmines and Harold W. Stanley, "The Transformation of the New Deal Party System: Social Groups, Political Ideology, and Changing Partisanship among Northern Whites, 1972–1988," *Political Behavior* 14 (1992): 213–37.

15. Ibid.

16. A score of "mean partisan difference" within groups was constructed by computing the average difference between mean positions (on a scale rang-

ing from 0 to 100) of Republican identifiers versus Democratic identifiers within the group over time. The mean partisan difference from 1956 to 1992 on social welfare issues was 18.6 within the upper-income group, 17.1 within the lower-income group, 13.7 among southern whites, and 17.7 among northern white Protestants.

17. The mean partisan difference on racial issues in 1956 and 1960 was 1.0 among upper-income respondents, −2.7 among lower-income respondents, −3.8 among southern whites, and 2.2 among northern white Protestants. The mean partisan difference on racial issues from 1964 through 1992 was 13.2 among upper-income respondents, 10.9 among lower-income respondents, and 7.0 among northern white Protestants. The mean partisan difference on racial issues among southern whites from 1964 through 1992 was 3.6.

18. See Layman, "Parties and Culture Wars."

19. The mean partisan difference on social and cultural issues from 1972 through 1992 was 5.9 for upper-income respondents, 6.0 for lower-income respondents, 1.9 for southern whites, and 7.2 for northern white Protestants. The mean partisan difference on social and cultural issues before 1980 was 0.2 for upper-income respondents, 1.0 for lower-income respondents, −.9 for southern whites, and −2.2 for northern white Protestants. From 1980 through 1992, the mean partisan difference on these issues was 8.7 for upper-income respondents, 8.5 for lower-income respondents, and 11.8 for northern white Protestants. The mean partisan difference for southern whites over this period was only 3.2.

20. Alan I. Abramowitz, "It's Abortion, Stupid: Policy Voting in the 1992 Presidential Election," paper presented at the annual meeting of the American Political Science Association, Washington, D.C., 1993; and Layman, "Parties and Culture Wars."

Thomas B. Edsall

The Cultural Revolution of 1994:
Newt Gingrich, the Republican Party,
and the Third Great Awakening

PREPARING THIS ESSAY has been a pleasure because American politics has become more interesting and more uncertain than at any point in recent memory. The country appears to be in the midst of an upheaval that will change the assumptions and language of politics as they have evolved from roughly the height of the civil rights movement in the mid-1960s to the presidential election of 1992.

At a minimum, the basic premise that the natural inclination of the American electorate is to send a Democratic majority to Congress simply does not hold. By every measure I can think of—energy, campaign contributions, control of the public agenda, the strength of the core coalition, intellectual vigor, aggressiveness—the Republican Party at the moment is driving the political debate in America. Samuel Lubell, who chronicled the development of the Democratic Party's New Deal Coalition, used to describe the Democratic Party as the energy-generating sun of American politics, and the Republican Party as the moon, dependent on the reflected light of the opposition. That sun-moon relationship has been reversed, and the consequences for both the culture and politics of the United States are enormous.

Five Forces for Change

One of the prime movers in contemporary American political culture is Newt Gingrich, and if he has any peculiarity, it is an affection for making lists. The trouble with lists is that they are never adequate; something is always left off. But in the light of Gingrich's success in changing the face of Washington, D.C., let me start off with a list of my own, and argue that American politics is being driven by the collision of five forces:

❑ The first of these forces is the erosion and discrediting of the political and cultural left and of postwar American liberalism. The reasons for this are complex, and I try to explore some of what is at work later on, but the direct political consequence has been the severe wounding of the legitimacy of the Democratic Party.

❑ The second force consists of the ascendance of a Republican Party and of a conservative leadership stratum. The Republican Party has been a major beneficiary of the globalization of economic competition. Traditional Democratic policies of protecting workers through domestic programs no longer work effectively when the nation's borders are porous—permitting the increasingly unregulated flow of money and people—and when international market competition engulfs all domestic strategies.

These circumstances create a climate that now favors an ideology emphasizing a vigorous individualism, with both its positive dimension of personal responsibility and its negative dimension of unbridled self-interest. In other words, American politics is now operating in an environment in which market forces are seen as the honest broker of economic outcomes, an environment in which the burden falls back on the individual to assume responsibility for his or her success or failure.

The revival of individual responsibility built around a shift from Democratic interventionist economics to Republican market-based economics—a shift of infinitesimal magnitude by European standards but profoundly influential on the outlook of American voters—has in turn created the ideal conditions for the bridging of cultural and economic conservatism. In this, the ascendancy of the Republican Party has been driven in large part by the emergence of an assertive religiosity in politics, carrying with it a moral, social, and cultural conservatism unprecedented in American public life in this century.

By far the most important organizational development in American politics over the past decade has been the mobilization of the Christian Right, and the formation of the grassroots evangelical activist network known as the Christian Coalition. The culture of politics is driven by power. At the moment, the rise of the Christian Right in America has given momentum and power to the insistence on the restoration of a traditional social and moral order, an insistence that characterizes, for example, the current drive to reform welfare. This spirit of moral reformation in many respects stands in opposition to the postwar epoch of cultural, moral, social, and racial liberalism, a liberalism emphasizing first an expressive individualism and second an expanding set of legally secured, government-underwritten rights.

❐ The third major force structuring American politics is the continuing struggle to deal with the issue of race. Race pervades almost every aspect of American politics, most often in ways that are left unsaid. It is impossible to do justice to this issue in this brief note, but let me just touch on some points.

First and foremost, a profound ambiguity marks the racial attitudes of white Americans. There is, on the one hand, the collision of

THOMAS B. EDSALL

American egalitarian principles with a history of slavery and de jure racial segregation, and on the other a heavily black underclass that captures at the extreme the perceived erosion of the quality of American life. On the other side of this racial coin is the demonstrated willingness of white Americans to support black officials and candidates who share their work ethic and family values. This white hunger for black success and participation underpins the groundswell of support for Colin Powell, for example, and it has emerged in the election of a number of centrist black politicians in majority-white communities, ranging from Denver, Colorado, and Seattle, Washington, in the West to Rochester, New York, and Jacksonville, Florida, on the east coast.

In other words, black America has in many ways become the political repository of white anxieties, hopes, ambitions, and fears. In the years leading up to the enactment of the Civil Rights Act of 1964 and the Voting Rights Act of 1965, the issue of race empowered liberalism and the Democratic Party. In the years since then, race has been a major source of power for conservatism and the Republican Party. The issues of crime, welfare, and illegitimacy have in the past served as unexplored sources of white anger, anger sometimes freighted by racial antagonism. Now these issues are all before Congress in combination with the divisive topic of affirmative action and quotas. The conflicts and tensions surrounding these issues, which had in the past been muted and held silent, are now surfacing with a vengeance. The outcome in the immediate future appears sure to be a retrenchment in programs geared to the poor and to minorities.

❐ The fourth force driving American politics is the breakdown of traditional definitions of gender. The past thirty years have produced a revolution in the workplace, at home, and in bed. These trends have turned men, particularly white men, into powerful agents of conservatism, mainstays of the rightward movement of American politics. For many—but by no means all—men, the past three decades have been years of lost sexual and gender identity, and lost centrality in the culture. The major rights movements on behalf of women, minorities, and gays have often identified as a common adversary the heterosexual white man. For American men of all races, the past twenty years have been marked by declining or stagnant wages for the majority, by the collapse of a market in jobs paying high wages for a strong back, and by the steady collapse of the patriarchal family, with father as the breadwinner and mother as the caregiver.

❏ The fifth force in American politics concerns the economic dilemma: the crisis of jobs, wages, and American prosperity. Is the United States poised on the cusp of an era of continued global economic success, driven by a mastery of high technology? Or is the United States at the end of empire, caught in a downward spiral driven by the export of semi- and unskilled jobs to low-wage countries, and by the multinationalization of world commerce?

Together, these five forces have produced an ascendant conservatism in which the pivotal role of the evangelical right has profoundly influenced the character of politics, giving the entire center-right of the political spectrum the tone and tenor of a religious revival.

Conservative Strategy in a Changing Environment

There is no doubt that the Republican Party, under the guidance of its dominant figure, Newt Gingrich, remains closely tied to business and to the economic elite. These ties are recognized by the public, but for the moment at least, they do not constitute the kind of liability that the links to corporate America did for the GOP throughout the previous two generations. Instead, one of the central appeals of the Republican Party to the electorate—an appeal that, again for the moment, has not been wounded by the party's ties to American business—is that the party has become the vehicle for a moral reformation.

Crucial to maintaining this moral ascendancy has been the development by Gingrich and virtually all his allies in the House of Representatives of a strategy of purposefully demonizing the Democratic Party, with a fervor that has not been a part of American politics at least in recent memory. During the House debate in the spring of 1996 over welfare reform, for example, Republican Robert Walker, one of Gingrich's closest friends, painted a picture of the Democratic Party as a corrupt, morally bankrupt entity, determined to impose failure on America at large:

> What the Democrats are defending with their harsh, unreal, and irresponsible talk are programs that are immoral and corrupt. It is immoral to take money from decent, middle-class Americans who work for everything they have and give it to people who think they are owed the money for doing nothing.... It is immoral to consign poor people to lives of living hell as government dependents so that politicians and bu-

reaucrats can maintain power. . . . It is corrupt to pick on the most vulnerable people in our society, the children and the poor, to maintain one's own political power base. Yet that is what this debate has revealed about the opponents of welfare reform. They cannot accept good welfare reform because it changes the pattern of power in America. The immoral and corrupt system they have fostered comes to an end. What the Democrats speak on this floor is the language of fear—fear of the future, fear of change, and fear of the loss of their political power.[1]

The climate setting the stage to make this kind of demonization possible in November 1994, and for the months that followed, was created by the intersection of underclass deterioration and middle-class anguish. The continuing deterioration of the bottom rungs of American society—the underclass—began abruptly to accelerate in the mid- to late-1980s in ways that increasingly reverberated in politics. Receiving the most publicity was the surge in the number of shootings by young men. Starting in 1985, when crack cocaine became widely accessible, the murder rate among boys ages ten to fourteen and adolescents between the ages of fifteen and twenty shot up, more than doubling between 1985 and 1992. For young black men between the ages of fourteen and seventeen, the murder rate nearly tripled. The randomness of the violence and the threat inflicted on innocent bystanders by drive-by shootings, along with the assassination of drug dealers operating on playgrounds, changed the public character of homicide in the United States.

Less highly publicized, but integral to the sense of social decay, was an abrupt increase in the number of people on welfare. Through the 1980s, the number of people on welfare remained relatively constant at 10.5 million. Starting in 1989, this number began steadily to rise, breaking 13 million in 1992. There are complex reasons for this increase, including the recession of 1990–91, along with a rise in the number of households headed by single, never-married women—the group most likely to go on welfare. But the reasons are less important than the political impact of these changes, and the impact was to reinforce the notion that—modest as it is by British standards—the American welfare state had run amok. The combination of the availability of welfare, the lost stigmatization of welfare dependency, and the parallel destigmatization of out-of-wedlock pregnancy had created a dynamic that enlarged the scope of the welfare population in the United States.

An additional aspect of crisis in the American underclass lies in the continuing rise in the rate of illegitimacy. All underclass issues have, in the United States, a strong racial subtext, but in this case the most striking rate of increase has been among whites. Conservative analyst Charles Murray, who in the policy arena has played as major a role as Gingrich has in the political arena, touched the nerve end of this issue when he pointed out that the white rate of illegitimacy in 1991—at 22 percent of live births—was exactly what the black rate of illegitimacy was in 1964, when Daniel Patrick Moynihan in his controversial report warned of the collapse of the black family.

The conservative wing of the Republican Party has long recognized that social disorder is the Achilles heel of the Democratic Party. If the United States is in the process of an ongoing realignment, shifting power from the Democratic Party to the Republican Party, that process began in the elections of 1966 and 1968, when support for the Democratic Party collapsed—with surging crime rates, a wave of riots in major American cities, escalating illegitimacy rates, and the sudden near-doubling of welfare dependency in the midst of a growing economy.

More recently, in virtually every speech and interview before and after the 1994 election, Newt Gingrich repeated this line: "It is impossible for a civilization to survive with 12-year-olds having babies, 15-year-olds killing each other, 17-year-olds dying of AIDS, and 18-year-olds getting diplomas they can't read." In the political vision articulated by Gingrich, a central agent of these ills is the Democratic Party's "bureaucratic welfare state." To continue to quote the House Speaker, "the core assumptions of the bureaucratic welfare state are hopeless and destructive of human beings."[2]

In voicing this harsh assessment of contemporary liberalism in the United States and of the political arm of liberalism, the Democratic Party, Gingrich was not simply articulating a partisan portrayal of the opposition. Increasing percentages of voters in the United States have developed less a conclusion than a wary concern that the mainstay of contemporary American liberalism, the revolution in rights, has had the unintended consequence of undermining the capacity of adults to take responsibility for their own behavior and the capacity of children to mature into responsible adults.

What has happened to American politics, in effect, is that they have become moralized. American culture has always been characterized by a powerful moral tenor in the broad consensual support for the Protestant work ethic and the acceptance of the obligations of individualism. The difference now is that the American brand of conservatism has come to see government as a powerful agent shaping the national morality. The power of government to act as a force undermining personal morality has been a part of American conservatism for a long time. What has changed more recently is the development of the notion of government as an evangelical, positive force to raise the level of individual morality.

This premise underpins not only welfare reform, but issues as diverse as the pending reform of the legal system, the constitutional amendment for a balanced budget, proposed changes to prison policy designed to make life tough for convicted felons, and the drive to restore the teaching of values in the public school system. For the moment, this whole process of the political system turning inward, reviving personal responsibility and taking on the character of a religious revival, has precluded credible consideration of Democratic interventionist approaches to the economic issues that continue to worry voters.

Liberal Responses to Conservative Strategies

The most important of these issues has been the stagnation, and in many cases the decline, of weekly wages, and thus a growing inequality of income and wealth. In normal circumstances, these trends would favor the Democratic Party, but these are not normal circumstances. Instead, for the moment, wage stagnation and inequality have intensified the inclination toward placing responsibility on the shoulders of individuals for their condition, rather than on government or social policies.

Part of the logic of this is that the very nature of what economics and social class imply in the United States is undergoing a major reevaluation, and the new analyses lend themselves to conservative interpretation. Instead of viewing the position of an individual on the social and economic ladder as the outcome of a class order, the growing trend is to view class and social standing as determined by personal behavior, intelligence, and values. During the past twenty years, educational attainment has become much more influential in determining wages than it had been in the past. In addition, there is a growing body of work showing that fatherlessness—father absence—resulting not from death but from either divorce or irresponsible paternity, has a profoundly damaging effect on the earnings and life course of children.

The argument can be (and has been) made that the driving force behind the collapse of families is the disappearance of good jobs in the cities where the worst-off Americans are concentrated. The more dominant view, however, is that the loss of manual and unskilled jobs interacts catalytically with the combination of government policies encouraging single motherhood, paternal irresponsibility and a lack of initiative, and individuals ill equipped to negotiate unrestrained free-market competition.

My own view is that the United States is now in the process of coming to terms with the costs of the rights revolution, costs that under Democratic Party liberalism were neither anticipated nor confronted, much less given adequate recognition in public discourse. The surge of interest in identity politics—the quest for self-knowledge and self-actualization—that characterized much of American (and European) liberalism in the 1960s and 1970s did result in lost community and family, and the repercussions of those losses are now playing out in the political system. In a recent essay on crime, the conservative social policy analyst James Q. Wilson put part of this into perspective when he wrote:

> Prosperity, freedom, and mobility have emancipated people almost everywhere from those ancient bonds of custom, family, and village that once held in check both some of our better and many of our worst impulses. The power of the state has been weakened, the status of children elevated, and the opportunity for adventure expanded; as a consequence, we have experienced an explosion of artistic creativity, entrepreneurial zeal, political experimentation—and criminal activity.[3]

The costs accompanying creativity, innovation, and experimentation have encompassed far more than criminal activity, to include for many, especially those in the bottom half of the income distribution, lost family, community, and social authority and prestige. But the contemporary upheavals of the political system also reflect in large part the continuing energy and vitality of the United States, a capacity to respond to the changing social, economic, and cultural marketplace with enterprise and innovation.

I would like to conclude this essay on a personal note. I have spent thirty years covering politics in America, and most of the time my sense of the future has been pessimistic. The political changes that have taken place, particularly the inclination of the right to make moral judgments on the less successful, are often disturbing. More threatening to the structure of democratic values in the United States is the possible emergence of a strong and intolerant *populism* of the right, the kind of populism that has a dark history in the United States and a violent history in Europe—the kind of populism currently reflected in the growth of antigovernment militias in a number of states and the tragic bombing in Oklahoma City.

The anger and violence characterizing white and black extremes in the United States are evident tests of the capacity of the American political system to achieve ideological and racial integration in fulfillment of the competitive egalitarianism on which the country was founded, tests of the capacity to achieve an integration of both community and creativity, of innovation and responsibility. It appears now that governments on both sides of the Atlantic, in Britain and in the United States, will attempt to take on the task of social integration in a period of globalized economic transactions and expanding democratized rights. While not identical, the substance of public debate in Britain and the United States is at least strikingly similar—the growth of means-tested programs, government corruption, crime, deindustrialization, inequality, immigration, and the crisis of funding for the welfare state.

Where the electorates of the two countries are diverging, however, is in their political response. The voters in Britain are on the verge of entrusting the debate to the party of the left, while in the United States, the voters in 1994 signaled a preference for the party of the right. Together, the two countries, as well as all the developed democracies, will test the boundaries of democratic governance: in dealing with the conflicts between social justice, wealth generation, individual obligation, public order, poverty, political equality, and evolving notions of the complete self and the well-lived life.

Governments of all kinds are under intensified pressure to find ways to resolve increasingly various and complex conflicts while maintaining some form of legitimacy. As crucial elements of this process, Britain and the United States are now on the verge of initiating new trials, of liberalism of the left especially, the outcome of which will help determine the vitality and strength of democratic governance itself in a time of political, social, and economic revolution.

Notes

1. "Personal Responsibility Act of 1995," *Congressional Record,* 21 March 1995, H3352 ff.

2. "Address on the First One Hundred Days of the New Republican Congress," nationally televised, 7 April 1995; see also Jonathan D. Salant, "Gingrich Sounds Familiar Themes," *Congressional Quarterly Weekly Report,* 8 April 1995, 981.

3. James Q. Wilson, "What To Do about Crime," *Commentary* 98 (September 1994), 26.

COALITIONS

Byron E. Shafer

"We Are All Southern Democrats Now":
The Shape of American Politics
in the Very Late Twentieth Century

T HE STRUCTURE OF American politics, the main factors that shaped politicking in the United States, became more complicated during the postwar years. And the same can be said for the issue context, the substance, of that politics. Joel Silbey, Charles Jones, and Alan Ehrenhalt have illuminated major aspects of structure. Michael Barone, Edward Carmines, and Thomas Edsall have done the same for main elements of substance. In truth, however, all move back and forth between substance and structure, between issues and the politicking around them, as any broad-gauge interpretation would have to do. Any concluding effort to knit these pieces together must, in turn, do the same.

One strategy for such an effort is to begin with the social coalitions that characterized American politics across this period. From one side, these coalitions both shaped and were shaped by the central substantive concerns of their time. Different social groups preferred different outcomes on particular issues, so it was not possible to mobilize the same coalitions across all issues or to staple all new issues on the same old coalitions. From the other side, these coalitions were both gathered by and energized the political parties, those key intermediaries of American politics that linked public wishes to governmental institutions. Again, some coalitions were more easily accommodated by one party, some by the other; just as one party or the other was more or less inherently stressed by various coalitional alternatives.

The Late New Deal Era

With one very major exception, the two social coalitions characterizing American politics when the postwar period began were built along lines of social class.[1] There was a blue-collar coalition, which found its institutional home in the national Democratic Party and was composed of working-class Americans generally, the poor, plus a few other religious and ethnic minorities. And there was a white-collar coalition, which found *its* institutional home in the national Republican Party and was composed of middle-class Americans generally, along with northern and western farmers. The New Deal—the coming of the welfare state—had been responsible for changing an old politics in which these coalitions had been primarily sectional and cultural into a new politics in which social class was the main organizing principle, and Democratic management of the pursuit of World War II had then kept these locked into place for the duration of the war.

The political parties on which these coalitions settled, as much through tactical opportunity and mutual discovery as through grand strategy, were actually at different places on what would become a common organizational continuum. The Democrats retained a number of the older big-city machines and managed to extend their operating procedures to the state level in some states, though much of the rest of the party had already given way to volunteer activist branches. The policy successes of the New Deal, especially its social insurance programs, actually further undermined old-fashioned party "machinery," but the popularity of these programs was such that popular identification with the Democratic Party remained strong. Indeed, as other (and more Republican) identifiers passed out of society, the Democratic share of the general public continued to expand; because the Democratic Party was still "where the action was," ambitious newcomers to politics continued to flow disproportionately into it as well.

The Republicans, by contrast, had not just been forced back into their core geographic areas by the policy successes of the New Deal and by the newly enlarged Democratic coalition. They were forced back, within these areas, on established party officeholders, so the formal structure of the official party was simultaneously more consequential than that of the Democrats and more skeletal, that is, in possession of fewer regular party workers. Those Republican officials who had remained in place, often through the depression and World War II, were still principally motivated by opposition to the New Deal. A successful standard-bearer such as Dwight Eisenhower could temporarily finesse this; a disastrous standard-bearer like Barry Goldwater would exaggerate it.

The greatest exception to all of this, an exception that would prove pivotal at any number of points across the postwar years, was the American South. The New Deal did add social welfare issues to southern politics; indeed, the main social insurance programs of the New Deal were overwhelmingly popular there. But this remained an overlay. The New Deal did not bring class-based coalitions to this region, and it remained monolithically Democratic, as it had been since the American Civil War. In such a world, the old courthouse rings of the rural South continued to hold great organizational sway. Moreover, the presence of a total class structure in one party gave the resulting southern Democrats a much more moderate cast than their northern or western counterparts. They would thus have been a reliably dissident wing of the national Democratic Party even if it had not been for the existence of explicit—legal—racial segregation, which was also an organizing principle of the southern democracy.

Together, these social coalitions, along with their issue preferences and their organizational principles, gave a distinctive pattern to partisan politicking, most easily seen through its electoral incarnation. This pattern was to unravel only slowly across the postwar years.[2] Politics thus remained centered on social welfare issues, on attempts to ensure a full-employment economy and to add the "missing pieces" of the New Deal, the ones that had been enunciated but not implemented in the 1930s. It was not that such policies necessarily carried the day, year in and year out. It was just that conflict over their *substance* was a reliable electoral benefit to the national Democratic Party. The Republicans did, however, benefit from a modest but consistent perception that they were better at handling foreign affairs. The Democrats never consciously conceded this realm during these years, so there was no great policy difference between the parties. Yet when foreign policy managed to displace social welfare at the center of public concern, especially when this was coupled with the corruption scandals that seemed endemic to long-running partisan dominance, the Republicans could disrupt established Democratic control.

All of which was powerfully buttressed by the place of the great interest groups, of corporate business and, especially, organized labor. While the New Deal was being implemented, labor was becoming the great organized interest supporting the national Democratic Party. The immediate postwar years were the high point of its aggregate numbers, its geographic reach, and its economic resources. Indeed, labor organization often went so far as to substitute for the declining machinery of the official Democratic Party. The organizational counterpart to this within the Republican Party was not really corporate business but small business, and a hostility both to social welfare programs and to the taxes necessary to fund them remained substantively central to small business sectors of the party. Nevertheless, corporate Republicans, through the provision of "blue-ribbon" candidates and of financial support, played an important indirect role. Moreover, they were the organizational mainstay of any efforts to reach an accommodation with the substance of the New Deal.

Accordingly, when the corporate wing of the Republican Party found itself a presidential candidate, as it did with Eisenhower, *and* when he was self-evidently able to capitalize on foreign policy as an issue, as Eisenhower was, these were years in which the coming of a Republican presidency also implied the coming of unified Republican control of national government. Corporate Republicans and their sympathizers, however, were not a main influence on Republican congressmen across the nation—*their* hearts belonged to the small business wing—so that even under Eisenhower, a return to the politics of "rolling back the New Deal" quickly swept the Republican majority out of Congress. More commonly, in any case, organized labor and the regular Democratic Party resolved their differences around a unifying candidate, most often through the aid of social welfare issues. And that candidate and his party then appeared as the "natural" owners of government.

The Era of Divided Government

That arrangement—the interaction of substantive issues, social coalitions, and party structures—attenuated gradually as the postwar years passed. Yet despite its gradualist character, the end of this arrangement is easy to date. The election of 1964 was still a classic incarnation of the late New Deal order; the election of 1968 inaugurated what we have come to know as the "era of divided government." Somewhere between these two elections, then, a set of cumulative structural changes and cumulative issue shifts produced a new political order. Its hallmark, uninterpretable at the time but diagnostic after the fact, was a partisan pattern: Republicans capture the presidency without even threatening to capture Congress. But a new and much more complex set of social coalitions was really the heart of this change, once again linking—affecting and affected by—the substance of political issues from one side and the structure of political parties from the other.[3]

Some things did not change. Social welfare issues continued to divide the parties in familiar ways, and they continued to divide them strongly. The public continued to support the main social insurance programs of Franklin Roosevelt's New Deal (unemployment insurance, Social Security), and that public went on to integrate new programs from Lyndon Johnson's Great Society (Head Start, Medicare) into this ongoing liberal consensus. Moreover, these economic and social welfare concerns continued to be the basis for *party identification* within the general public, so economic and welfare liberals were Democrats and economic and welfare conservatives were Republicans, and the Democratic Party remained the majority party in public affections.

What was different, then, was an increased polarization on issues of foreign affairs, additionally stressing the two-party coalitions and cumulatively benefiting the Republicans overall. What was also different—even more different—was the arrival of a whole array of previously unpoliticized "cultural" issues, dealing with the social character of American life. Crime and punishment, educational policy, the public role of religion, childrearing practices, abortion, public protest: all these gave life to a general concern that had previously seemed consensual and had largely been kept outside of politics.

In the case of foreign affairs, increased polarization, in the wake of the Vietnam war and as the Democratic Party pulled back from containment and anticommunism, emphasized tensions that had always been incipiently present in the two great social coalitions. Here the liberal coalition on social welfare was not the same—it was effectively unrelated to—the liberal (the accommodationist) coalition on foreign affairs. Just as the conservative coalition on social welfare was unrelated to—effectively at right angles to—the conservative (the nationalist) coalition on foreign affairs. As a result, when foreign affairs was the issue of concern, many social welfare liberals, normally Democratic in their preferences, should have preferred (and did prefer) the *anti*-social welfare party, the Republicans.

This situation, noteworthy as it was, remained modest by comparison to the situation on the newly politicized cultural issues of American politics. Once again, the two policy coalitions in this realm, the liberal and the conservative coalitions, were strikingly different from the two counterpart coalitions on social welfare. The liberal (the progressive) coalition on these issues was as likely to be conservative as liberal on social welfare or economics generally. Conversely, the conservative (the traditionalist) coalition on issues involving cultural values was as likely to be liberal as conservative on issues of social welfare or economics. The issue substance of American politics was, accordingly, much more complex, as was the political party structure shaping the politicking around this newly complicated issue context.

This situation did not appear to result principally from a polarization on the part of the general public, precipitating a new and cross-cutting issue universe to challenge the political parties. Instead, structural changes within the parties themselves generated a polarized and cross-cutting set of *policy options* for the general public.[4] The Republican Party had actually moved earlier to a modern party structure, whereby the formal machinery was run by shifting networks of independent issue activists, motivated by intense but particular substantive concerns. Yet the Democratic Party too had come a long way down that road by the time of the 1968 elections. Initial attempts to see that the Democratic disasters of 1968 were not repeated then effectively dispossessed the residual incumbents of a formal hierarchy of party offices, incumbents who were also the final link to the preferences and principles of the late New Deal era.

In their place, again, came the independent issue activists, and it was this development that completed (and institutionalized) the new arrangement. For, in fact, Democratic activists were no longer much moved by the main issues that created overall Democratic majorities in the public at large, namely, social welfare and especially social insurance issues. Instead, they were moved secondarily by foreign affairs and principally by cultural values. This did not produce a new —and simple—polarization to American politics, however, reflecting a sharply but simply altered social alignment, because it was *not* mirrored directly on the Republican side. There were, undeniably, new cultural and international activists in the Republican Party too, and they were uniformly conservative. But the old main motivation for internal Republican politics, of cutting taxes even if it meant cutting programs, remained the dominant motivating theme for most Republican Party workers—remaining perfectly comfortable for the new cultural conservatives as well.

All of which went a long way toward explaining electoral outcomes in the new political era.[5] Or, at least, Republican presidents with Democratic Congresses were a logical product of a politics with conservative majorities on cultural values and foreign affairs, liberal majorities on social welfare and economics generally. The presidency could never escape these underlying cross-pressures, being nationally elected, and that fact alone vastly improved Republican prospects in the office. But the presidency, thanks to its great symbolic potential, was also an obvious policy focus for concerns with foreign affairs, as well as for cultural values.

By contrast, Democratic majorities in the public at large could continue, thanks to a continuing social welfare liberalism. When there was unified partisan control of government, it was much more likely to be in Democratic hands. Yet even when there was not, a continuing social welfare liberalism could easily be registered in the main local agents of American politics, in its senators but especially its congressmen. Moreover, most congressional districts were sufficiently homogeneous in social terms that *cross-pressures* from foreign affairs or cultural values did not reliably intrude and could be much less stressfully addressed when they did. Democratic Congresses, even in the absence of a Democratic president, remained the norm.

Once more, the American South required special attention within this overall matrix. On the one hand, and at long last, the South underwent tremendous economic development across the postwar years, bringing class politics (among other things) to the one region where it had been suppressed for a hundred years. Liberal Democrats—real, genuine, "northern" Democrats—appeared in its industrialized areas. Simultaneously, a real Republican Party—"national" Republicanism—appeared as well, aimed at winning and governing and not just at managing federal patronage. Yet all this occurred while the rest of the nation was shifting from the late New Deal era to the era of divided government. Moreover, *this* shift was to be particularly intense within the American South.

This was true in general terms, given that the South was reliably nationalist in foreign affairs, reliably and deeply traditionalist in cultural values. It was true in specific and pointed terms because the South was where the practices of legal segregation had to be forcibly dismantled, practices reaching into every aspect of life. Yet the challenge of national shifts in the partisan politics of these issues was intensified by a continuing southern support for social insurance programs. And it was compounded, of course, by that long-running Democratic predominance, now being shattered and reorganized by economic development. As a result, while the rest of the nation was undergoing the kind of major political change that occurs perhaps once every half-century, the South was undergoing two such changes at the same time.

The larger result, nationwide, was a partisan world in which Republican presidents facing Democratic Congresses became commonplace. It was a world where unified Democratic control of government was the most common partisan option. It was a world where discontent with a Democratic president could now reasonably be expressed by split-partisan control in the other direction: a Democratic president facing a *Republican* Congress. And it was a world where the remaining option, unified Republican control, was surely back on the table. Nevertheless, these were not the crucial—the defining—characteristics of a new order. They were instead just manifestations of those defining characteristics, of which there were three:

❏ Stable and cross-cutting policy preferences within the general public on the main issues of their time.
❏ Stable policy offerings from the two major parties, neither of which matched the overall national preferences.
❏ Shifting social coalitions at the grassroots, evolving into shifting party coalitions within national government.

Budgetary Politics in 1990

The same contours—for social coalitions, their issue substance, and the associated party structure—may seem less easy to isolate for institutional (as opposed to electoral) politicking. Institutions admittedly add their own specific twists to the political process, and individual pieces of legislation reflect underlying influences in ways specific to their particular substance. Moreover, the mechanics of legislating normally involve *compromises,* across several institutions and even across several issues. Nevertheless, ongoing social coalitions do not thereby disappear. Nor do continuing public majorities in general issue areas. Nor, finally, do the ways in which one or the other, or both, political parties institutionalize social coalitions and issue positions.

Moreover, there is a category of political conflicts, almost always major, which is especially good at stripping away the surface twists and turns of institutional politicking, to reveal the ongoing contours of a political order beneath. These are the handful of major issues in any period that become central to politics not because they are chosen by major actors—presidents, senators, congressmen, or the governing or the opposition party—but because they are forced in by the environment. They are thus substantial policy priorities, demanding attention from most major actors. Yet they are, by definition, not initiated by the tactical choices of any of the main players. They ought therefore to be particularly good at eliciting grander and deeper influences, influences to which political tacticians must themselves adapt but which they have not been able to shape in the first instance.

There were in fact two such issues, and crises, during the Bush presidency, in the period between the end of one election campaign and the beginning of another: the budget conflict of 1990 and the Gulf War. Both were, albeit in different ways, very much "forced in" by the world outside ongoing policy conflict. In addition, each reinforces *half* the lessons of an electoral analysis of the era of divided government. Together, then, they make the same composite points in an institutional context. And between them, the one that history is likely to forget, the budget fiasco of 1990, was actually to prove the more accurate harbinger of the electoral conflicts of 1992.

Before that, however, the election of 1988 had been an archetypal contest for the era of divided government in almost the opposite sense.[6] Which is to say that the environment had imposed no obvious issue priorities on the campaign, and the two parties had been free to offer orthodox versions of their standard themes as a result. Not surprisingly, the Republicans focused on foreign affairs and cultural values, while the Democrats countered with social welfare and economic benefit. This was probably enough to produce a stereotypical outcome—a Republican president facing a solidly Democratic Congress—especially given that the Republicans hit very hard on cultural values and benefited from generally good economic conditions, while the Democrats came late to their main social welfare themes and blurred their usual message on group identifications. In any case, the outcome was truly stereotypical: a solid Republican win for George Bush as president, with an actual gain by the Democrats of one Senate and three House seats in Congress!

The policy story of the first year of the resulting Bush administration was not characterized by major issues arguably forced in by the environment outside national government. But at the end of the first financial quarter of 1990, Bush got the bad, private word from his economic policy advisers: the economy was slowing, and there was no longer any hope for growing out of the budget deficit. That was bad enough, but a growing deficit in a slowing economy also suggested that the budget-cutting provisions of the Gramm-Rudman-Hollings Act would kick in automatically later that year, inflicting true financial chaos on the government. Nevertheless, in an era of split partisan control, even edging away from his promise of "no new taxes" proved fraught with difficulties for the president.[7]

Inevitably, there was no active benefit in cutting programs or raising taxes, much less in doing both. But with each party in control of one branch of national government, each needed to get the other to take the necessary (and unpleasant) actions *before* it acted, so as not to risk paying all the costs, and perhaps ending up with no product anyway. In late April, then, Bush had his budget director, Richard Darman, call for White House/congressional talks on some new budget agreement. Bush himself remained quiet, however, and congressional leaders effectively ignored the offer.

Two weeks later, in mid-May, Bush personally weighed in, calling for a White House/congressional "summit," with no preconditions. The result—resonant for students of social coalitions, along with their issue substance and party linkages, but strangely anomalous to most other analysts—was not shock among the president's personal supporters, or shock among members of the opposition party. Instead, the shock came within his own party in Congress:

❐ For *presidential Republicans,* the logic was inescapable. In order to continue to control the presidency within the current political order, they needed to be sure that a presidential campaign did not center on economic concerns and social welfare matters. Bush was fully prepared to move away from the "no new taxes" pledge if it guaranteed that outcome.

❏ For *congressional Democrats,* the logic was equally attractive. In order to avoid automatic cuts to those programs that, after all, sustained *their* majority in Congress in the era of divided government, but especially because they might actually shift expenditures from defense to social programs and thus secure clear policy gains, they needed to seize this particular (and probably transient) opportunity. To that end, the Democratic congressional leadership was fully prepared to join President Bush.

❏ For *congressional Republicans,* however, the logic was radically different. Economic moderation and social welfare protection had nothing to offer them; what they had to offer on this dimension was the promise of holding the line on taxes. Naturally, they were outraged. One hundred Republican congressmen, speaking for an even larger collection of Republican congressional candidates, signed a letter scolding the president and asserting that any tax increase was "unacceptable."

The dilemma—the box—within which House Republicans in particular found themselves deserves emphasis. Being ideologically committed to the minority side of the energizing issue for party politics in the House, they had long since resigned themselves, strategically, to making incremental additions (and avoiding incremental losses) to an institutionalized minority. Within that context, any White House deal offered only the latter—further incremental losses—and they responded accordingly. Despite this response, White House negotiators, sometimes including the president; Democratic congressional leaders, from both houses; and Republican congressional *leaders* began an ongoing series of discussions on some grand compromise to control the deficit.

These talks continued throughout the summer, without the elusive deal. While they were grinding on, Iraq invaded Kuwait. For the budget summit, this invasion, by making defense cuts more difficult and by threatening the economy further, suggested that only the actual arrival of a Gramm-Rudman "sequester," by then estimated at a cut of over $100 billion, would force a deal. In anticipation of precisely that, the negotiators withdrew to Andrews Air Force Base in mid-September and actually produced a package, one that was in fact a major victory for the Republican White House. It sustained defense expenditures; it increased Medicare fees; and it raised only nuisance taxes, along with the gasoline tax.

Remarkably, despite a comprehensive leadership deal, the measure failed in the House (where new revenue measures must originate), and it failed ignominiously, 179–254. Perhaps more remarkably, only the dissident faction of the majority party, the southern Democrats, supported it, by 45–38. Still more remarkably, it was *House Republicans* who pulled the plug on the entire deal, in the ultimate tribute to their commitment to the minority position on economic welfare but in a response fully consistent with a continuing and institutionalized political order. They voted no, 71–105. In return, northern Democrats, who had never liked anything about the proposed package, joined House Republicans to kill the whole thing.

And at that point, congressional *Democratic* leaders, with impending Gramm-Rudman cuts looming as an aid to their efforts, seized control of the process. The president fell back to a reactive position, and Senate leaders sought to broker a deal, one that might be sold to more liberal colleagues in the House and to a more conservative president. If there had to be some package to contain the deficit (and shore up a Republican president), and if House Republicans would not cooperate, then congressional Democrats—especially Senate Democrats —were effectively entitled to write the relevant legislation.

This they did. They shifted cuts from domestic welfare to defense; they rejected a cut in the capital gains tax; and they finished by increasing income taxation in the upper brackets. Indeed, to the extent that they moderated their economic welfare preferences, it was to accommodate other Senate Democrats, not congressional Republicans and not even the president, who was left hanging, day by day, waiting to sign whatever they could construct. A successful ultimate vote necessarily reflected a national Democratic coalition on economics and social welfare, with maximum influence for the piece of that coalition, the southern Democrats, most needed to put this together. Accordingly, the final vote of 228–200 in the House was led by the southern Democrats, 61–20, followed by the northern Democrats, 120–54, and opposed by the Republicans, 47–126.

The Gulf War

Congress actually managed to adjourn from these negotiations with only days remaining in the fall congressional election campaign. And with only days remaining, polls showed the Republicans, already weak in Congress, facing a disaster—Congress being "about" social welfare and economic benefit, and the Republican Party having just highlighted itself as the party on the wrong side of these fundamental concerns. In a response fully reflecting the contours of the current political order, George Bush hit the campaign trail to talk about the *Gulf*, and about American values and their place in the world, where Republicans (not Democrats) have their established advantage.[8]

In the immediate sense, this effort was to be a failure. An already weak party managed to lose another Senate seat and eight more House seats, meaning that even a Bush landslide in 1992 was unlikely to provide the Republicans with a recapture of either the House or the Senate. If this failure held no hint of a larger shift in the existing order, it was because congressional Democrats were about to return every favor that Bush and his congressional partisans had given them over the preceding months. In so doing, they were also about to complete the institutional picture of a political order at work. For what congressional Democrats were in fact about to do was to seize on the Gulf conflict, to sketch *themselves* as the party out of step with the American public, and to rescue (at least temporarily) the personal popularity of George Bush. In the process, they were to exemplify, and energize, the great alternative pattern of social coalitions in modern American politics, and the great alternative pattern of partisan alliances that followed from it.

Iraq had seized Kuwait on 2 August. By 8 August, President Bush had introduced a major American troop presence, his "line in the sand." The usual rally in public opinion had followed, sufficient to stifle partisan conflict for a number of weeks. But by mid-September, as the prospects of immediate combat had receded, the partisan honeymoon had begun to ebb as well.[9] At first, Democratic congressional sniping at a Republican president came from both directions. On 17 September, the House Foreign Affairs Committee actually began the attack from the right, through hearings effectively organized around the question "Who lost Kuwait?" And on 18 September, the Foreign Operations Subcommittee of the House Appropriations Committee began the attack from the left, refusing an arms deal for Saudi Arabia *and* refusing to forgive Egypt's military debt.

Thereafter, however, and for the next four months, there was to be constant sniping, but all from the same general position, from the left, the accommodationist side of the issue. Seen one way, this merely reasserted "politics as usual" in the stereotypical and clichéd sense. But seen another way, what it really did was to reassert the normal politics of an established arrangement of coalitions, issues, and parties. Part of this, in turn, was a straightforward reflection of the dominant views of party elites. Thus Democratic elites were always unhappy with the notion of the use of force, a view expressed throughout this period in a demand for extended economic sanctions. But part of this reassertion was also entangled, as it must be in an era of split partisan control, with issues of institutional prerogative. How far *could* the president go, this Republican president, without seeking authorization from Congress, a *Democratic* Congress?

In the background of this question, by extension, was always the War Powers Act, which purported to limit the endangerment of American troops without congressional authorization but which remained untested, and nearly unacknowledged, by any American president. Within this environment, tactical politicking was to move back and forth. On 8 November, the president massively increased the number of American troops in the Middle East. On 20 November, congressional Democrats sued in federal district court to affirm that the president could not use these troops without congressional authorization. On 29 November, the United Nations authorized the use of force to remove Iraq from Kuwait. On 4 December, the House Democratic Caucus voted 177–37 that the president could not support this initiative without congressional approval.

The end of the Christmas recess and the coming of the 15 January deadline in the UN resolution finally forced the issue. Rather than face a basic constitutional conflict but unwilling to invoke the War Powers Act, the White House asked for congressional authorization of the use of force, an authorization granted under the constitutional provision (Art. I, sec. 8) giving Congress the power "to declare war." The debate on this was surprisingly powerful, venting what were, on one level, deeply felt and *personal* instincts about warfare and the national interest. Yet on a different level, this debate, like the vote to follow, was merely to register—to objectify, if you will—the current version of party alliances associated with continuing public majorities on major substantive concerns.

The result, most concretely, was a decision to go to war. Yet for students of the accompanying political order, two further things were effectively accomplished. First, congressional Democrats had put their party on the record, in both houses, as opposed to the use of force in the Gulf, a position consistent with internal elite preferences for at least the preceding quarter-century. But second, congressional Democrats, again in both houses, had provided the necessary votes for an authorization of the use of force, thereby reflecting not elite but underlying mass sentiment. The crucial House vote, where stronger party lines were thought to make the outcome most unclear, was 250–183, with Republicans 164–3, southern Democrats 53–32, and northern Democrats 33–147—roughly the same numbers as the vote on deficit reduction, but with different parties (and party factions) attached to them!

Seen one way, a nearly unbroken phalanx of Republicans had been joined by a sizable minority of Democratic defectors to adopt this declaration. Analyzed another way, an ongoing nationalist majority among the American public in foreign affairs had been registered in what had become the orthodox way, with a coalition of Republicans and southern Democrats defeating the northern Democratic Party. Presumably, either view guaranteed that the Democrats would acquire full blame if the war went well, no credit if it actually went badly. War did come, on 23 February, and did end, spectacularly, on 27 February. In response, Republican President George Bush moved from the low point of his presidential popularity, in the aftermath of the 1990 budget fiasco, to the high point of his—or perhaps any—presidential popularity, all within the space of four explosive months.

In the narrow chronology of these two major conflicts, as well as in the texture of their day-to-day politicking, the practical separation of the two issues may be their most distinctive feature. After a short period when potential Gulf expenditures threatened to dictate budget arrangements, budgetary politics unfolded in apparent disregard of developments in the Middle East. In the same way, in the aftermath of striking victories (and defeats) in budgetary maneuvering, neither Democratic nor Republican strategists showed any inclination to retailor their positions on the Gulf War, in order either to build on budgetary successes or to use the Gulf to make budgetary politics teach a different public lesson. On the surface, then, this practical separation was surprising.

Yet, on a deeper level, it would be more surprising if two such major crises actually managed not to reflect the larger order within which they played out, one that presumably linked them through its dominant characteristics. In fact, of course, this was not the case. For a different way to address the paradox of apparent independence for two such major, simultaneous issues—eliminating the paradox by making them fully interdependent and consistent at a deeper level—is just to note that each precisely reflected its piece of an overarching order, and the two pieces together reflected that order as a totality. Indeed, these two issues, together, contributed almost a checklist of key structural elements to the contemporary order: of social coalitions, substantive issues, and party alliances.

In this, their politics certainly suggested a continuing nationalist and traditionalist majority in foreign affairs and cultural values, represented first by a sense that American principles had been violated in the Gulf, then by solid support for the American military presence there. Just as this same focused period of crisis politics suggested a continuing liberal and activist majority on social welfare and service provision, represented by a consistent concern for protecting basic social programs and subsequently by a desire to tilt taxation in the progressive direction.

On the other hand, their politics also suggested a continuing—and discordant—menu of policy choices imposed on these social majorities by the political parties. The main party actors remained determined to have a Republican Party program that was conservative across both domains, and a Democratic Party program that was liberal across both. In so doing, they effectively insisted that party alliances, within Congress and across to the presidency, be altered, though this was the farthest thing from their intent, so as to reconcile all these social and substantive tensions.

Inevitably, the result was two very different winning partisan coalitions. Within these, southern Democrats were liberal on social welfare and conservative on foreign affairs. As a result, only southern Democrats should have expected to be on the majority side of both conflicts, and only southern Democrats were. Northern Democrats, by contrast, were liberal on social welfare but also liberal on foreign affairs. They should have contributed the bulk of the winners on deficit reduction and the bulk of the losers on the Gulf War, and again they did. Republicans, finally, were conservative in the two realms, entitling them to lose badly on the deficit and win decisively on the Gulf.

A different way to summarize the same situation, a way characterized by a good deal more asperity, would be to say that elite actors from each party had actually forced the conflict in exactly the issue domain where they should logically have expected to lose! Thus it was congressional *Republicans,* the group who most needed help on distributional (economic) matters, who created the conflict that rebounded so powerfully to their disadvantage on the budget. Just as it was congressional Democrats who created the conflict on foreign intervention, which rebounded so swiftly to *their* disadvantage on the Gulf.

Deficit Reduction in 1993

With the Gulf rather than the deficit still uppermost in their minds, many analysts (along with many party leaders, in truth) assumed that, the congressional elections of 1990 notwithstanding, President Bush himself could rely on easy reelection. This was not an unreasonable view on its own grounds—the Gulf was closer than the deficit to the vote—but it missed the real place of both the Gulf War *and* the deficit fiasco, not as particular influences on voting behavior, but as general indicators of underlying (and ongoing) public preferences.

It was not that people would be asked to choose retrospectively between one or the other. It was not even that either would have much direct role in the 1992 campaign, though the Gulf was to have clearly the larger role in that regard. It was rather that the deficit and the Gulf were reasonable incarnations—obvious surface expressions—for a set of underlying *and continuing* preferences among the American public. Accordingly, if foreign affairs were to be the dominant theme of 1992, then George Bush would surely be back. If fiscal priorities were to be the dominant theme, then the budget fiasco of 1990 was a far better guide to the underlying situation.

As indeed it proved to be.[10] Governmental response to a serious recession—the one, ironically, that Bush had tried to mitigate—became the main issue of the 1992 campaign, the one forced in by the larger policy environment. Thanks partly to fallout from this same recession and to deliberate efforts by the Clinton campaign, health care—one of the great social insurance programs—became the main secondary policy concern. And the Clinton presidency was a logical product. To add irony, however, the first environmentally imposed policy conflict of the incoming Clinton administration was to fall in the same realm as the first policy crisis of the outgoing Bush administration, namely, the continuing fiscal deficit and its appropriate resolution.

This outcome gained surface drama from the degree to which Clinton had consistently repudiated deficit reduction as a governmental priority. As an aspirant for the Democratic nomination, he had made economic growth and "good jobs" the centerpiece of his campaign. With the nomination secured, Clinton had moved these priorities into the Democratic platform, hammering them again in his acceptance speech. And in the fall campaign, he had been monotonous —brutal—in giving them a final affirmation, boiled down privately to the aphorism "it's the economy, stupid!" Not surprisingly, when the result was victory at the polls, Clinton announced his intention to begin with an economic-stimulus package.

Three factors were quickly to undo this year-long affirmation.[11] In the background was a change in the state of the economy, which had begun growing vigorously during the fourth quarter of 1992, albeit too late to rescue George Bush. In the foreground was the electoral showing of independent Ross Perot, amassing an impressive 19 percent of the vote through an assault on "politics as usual," as exemplified by the refusal of the two main parties to tackle the deficit. And in the middle, where these two influences met operationally, was Congress. Within it, southern Democrats were the group with perennial deficit concerns; they had actually been the faction most supportive of efforts by *George Bush* to address the deficit. But there was now a second group of concern, in the form of a large cohort of freshman Democrats from the North. Many had run in a policy environment shaped as much by Perot as by Clinton, and many had themselves campaigned on a promise to "do something" about this problem. All could read the November outcome—Clinton 43 percent, Bush 37 percent, and Perot 19 percent—as evidence that their own reelections might turn on progress, at least on the deficit issue.

What might have been an immediate collision between the president and his own party on Capitol Hill was nevertheless avoided by the sheer technical requirements of a program that promised job creation, investment incentives, deficit reduction, and middle-class tax cuts. By 20 February, when a comprehensive package was unveiled, the new president had recognized the difficult congressional environment, by linking economic stimulus to deficit reduction and by eliminating the promised tax cuts.

Within a week, priorities had perforce changed further. Congressional leaders discovered that they lacked the votes to pass a stimulus package in advance of some bill indicating serious concern with the deficit. So the president agreed to tackle the budget resolution first, thereby institutionalizing his targets for spending cuts and tax *increases*. Even then, further items of deficit reduction had to be added to the resolution before the more hesitant among Democrats on the House and Senate Budget Committees could close ranks behind it. But the necessary items were found, and straight party votes then brought the resolution out of both committees, through both houses, and on to the president for signature by the end of March.

A resolution was not actual deficit reduction, of course. That would have to come later, with the reconciliation bills. Nor, it quickly developed, was a resolution sufficient to save the stimulus package.

The House of Representatives had long offered the purest partisanship on economic/welfare matters, and the House did produce another party-line vote, sending the stimulus package to the Senate. The Senate Democratic leadership, however, began without even a majority for the stimulus plan until it added yet more spending cuts to firm up the southern Democrats. This majority then ran into a Republican filibuster, in part a response to the deliberately partisan strategy followed by the Democrats to date. And the effort to lift this filibuster through a coalition with moderate Republicans next ran, fatally, into the reforms from 1990.

As part of the 1990 fiscal resolution, Congress had decreed that any new spending had to be offset by cuts in the same general realm, unless the president cited a national economic emergency. Under normal conditions, if Clinton were to comply with this legislation, there would thus be precious little *net* economic stimulus. If he were to escape it, he needed to get moderate Republicans not only to join his policy coalition but to affirm that the nation required an "emergency special." In the event, this was asking too much, and the economic-stimulus plan died quietly during the Easter recess.

Having set out with deficit reduction as secondary to economic stimulus, the Clinton administration was left with deficit reduction as its sole possibility for an economic initiative. The main contours of *policy* conflict within this realm were identical to those that had surfaced in 1990: the balance between spending cuts and tax increases; the balance among cuts between entitlements and defense; the balance among taxes between progressivity and proportionality. Under the Constitution, the Clinton program had to visit the House first, but House politics was additionally complicated in 1993 by a fear among House Democrats that they would again be asked to rally to painful compromises proposed by the president, only to see him deal these away in negotiations with the Senate.

In the House, Chairman Dan Rostenkowski (D–Ill.) of the Ways and Means Committee nevertheless continued the previous partisan strategy of drafting compromises within the Democratic membership and then driving them through the full committee. The result was a classic northern Democratic package: favoring taxes over cuts, protecting entitlements rather than defense, preferring income taxes over levies on purchases. By the end of May, under extreme partisan pressure and still in fear of a Senate deal, the full House passed this measure by the narrowest of margins, 219–213, with all 175 Republicans voting no.

The centerpiece of the Clinton proposal, however, a comprehensive tax on the heat content of all fuels, known as the BTU tax, was already dying in the Senate while Rostenkowski was salvaging it in the House. Southern Democrats from energy-producing states defected first, cracking the Democratic majority while opening a huge revenue hole. These individuals then joined with moderate Republicans to propose a cap on entitlements, restoring the majority and reducing the hole. This move caused House Democrats, spearheaded this time by the Congressional Black Caucus, to withdraw *their* support, signaling the failure of this compromise in the House.

In a response remarkably parallel to the end-game in 1990, the president withdrew from direct involvement and allowed the Senate Democratic leadership to see if it could write a bill. Their proposal rebalanced Rostenkowski's main elements, minus the BTU tax, for which an increase in tax on gasoline and other transport fuels was substituted. That plan passed the Senate by the narrowest of margins, 50–49, depending on the tie-breaking vote of Vice-President Al Gore. Because there was still no reason to believe that this version would satisfy the House, the entire package came down to protracted negotiations in a conference committee during the month of August.

What emerged was a shift of Medicare caps, away from recipients and onto providers; further sharp cuts in defense spending; sharply higher income taxes in the upper brackets; and a nickel increase on the gasoline tax. The fate of all this remained every bit as shaky as previous compromises; votes were every bit as close; and their party-line character was every bit as prominent. The compromise passed the House by 218–216, with the Republicans again voting 0–175. It passed the Senate by 51–50, with Republicans voting 0–44 and Vice-President Gore again casting the decisive vote.

This bill was quickly signed by the president. The obvious result in its time was a measure that would define the fiscal policy of the Clinton administration, at least for the life of the 103d Congress. In that sense, and especially given its pure surface partisanship, it was a distinctly Clintonian document. But the result was also a remarkable set of parallels, in process and in outcome, with none other than the Bush administration of 1990. Moreover, those parallels go a long way toward exposing a continuing structure to American politics across these same years:

❐ Neither president began with any love for deficit reduction. George Bush addressed the issue in order to meliorate an economic downturn coinciding with what would be his bid for re-election. Bill Clinton addressed the issue in order to advance the economic-stimulus program that had been his main electoral theme—when the sharp recession feared by Bush did nevertheless occur.

❐ When forced to address the deficit, the two presidents began from roughly opposite positions, as befitted a Republican versus a Democratic incumbent on an economic issue. Bush sought a focus on cuts versus taxes; on entitlements versus defense among the cuts; on proportionality versus progression among the taxes. Clinton sought roughly the reverse.

❐ But at that point, they encountered a powerfully parallel political environment, conducing inevitably toward parallel results. Differences in the subsequent trajectory of politicking thus largely reflected different starting points for the two presidents; ultimate outcomes were still impressively similar, after all.

❐ Both presidents encountered entrenched and substantial Democratic majorities in the House and the Senate, majorities built on these very issues. But in truth, those Democratic majorities merely embodied continuing majorities in American public opinion, in support of social welfare benefits and of solidly progressive taxation.

❐ Both presidents thus had to build congressional majorities from the *same combination* of northern and southern Democrats, a fact masked by the difference between Bush's evident conflict with this potential majority and Clinton's conscious intention to make it his own.

❐ This outcome was buttressed, ultimately, by the obvious minority status of Republican *policy preferences* in this realm, and not just of congressional Republicans as a group—along with the intensity by which congressional Republicans held to these (minority) preferences.

When the result was remarkably similar in its policy content, that was variously surprising, ironic, or familiar, depending on whether the surface trajectory or the underlying structure was the main analytic focus.[12]

NAFTA

The North American Free Trade Agreement (NAFTA), destined to propel a second crisis vote onto the agenda of the Clinton administration within three months of the vote on deficit reduction, began life at the center of a web of trade policy calculations in the Bush administration. In substance, the proposal called merely for the addition of Mexico to a previous free-trade pact negotiated with Canada under President Ronald Reagan, thereby creating the "North American Free Trade Area." In its politics, on the other hand, NAFTA would attest once more to the continuity of a social coalition in a major policy area and of a set of partisan alignments embodying it, from the Bush through the Clinton administrations—albeit a very different set from that associated with deficit reduction.

Four aspects of American trade policy came together to generate NAFTA. The most general was a perception that the U.S.–Canada pact had indeed been a thorough success. The most specific was a request from the president of Mexico, Carlos Salinas de Gortari, that his country be added to the resulting free-trade zone. A third was the apparent progress of trade liberalization within the European Union, targeted on the symbolic date of 1992. And the fourth was the much more troubled progress of a revised and expanded General Agreement on Tariffs and Trade (GATT), the worldwide free-trade regime. President George Bush had always been philosophically in sympathy with free trade. NAFTA, accordingly, could be a means to advance this philosophy, a potential goad to GATT negotiators, and a partial protection against the worst case, where GATT failed but European economic integration proceeded.

The proposal had already encountered significant congressional opposition under Bush, surfacing the main concerns that would dog it thereafter. In the spring of 1991, Bush sought extension of the "fast-track provision," permitting a single up-or-down vote on the product of international trade negotiations. Opponents worried, not so much about GATT, as about possible job losses and environmental damage from a pact with Mexico. But these opponents were unable to separate fast-track authorization by geographic realm, and they were unwilling to be branded as all-purpose protectionists. In effect, what they did in the spring of 1991 was to suggest the further, deeper conflict likely when an actual agreement finally appeared.[13]

Bill Clinton, as an aspirant for the Democratic nomination, began his campaign with evident free-trade preferences too. As a southern Democrat, Clinton came out of the traditionally trade-oriented wing of his party. Moreover, as a candidate for the presidential nomination, Clinton's strategy was to present himself as a "new Democrat," supporting economic growth generally, along with the introduction of new technologies and a reduction in governmental regulation. As a successful nominee, on the other hand, he also inherited major party interests, not just the major environmental groups but especially organized labor, that had opposed the idea of NAFTA from the start.

His short-term strategy was to temporize, while allowing congressional Democrats to harass President Bush on the issue and otherwise emphasizing his economic-stimulus and health insurance programs. The conclusion of negotiations on the actual pact in mid-August, however, made this policy "straddle" increasingly difficult. From one side, congressional Democrats now called on him to promise to re-open negotiations. From the other side, candidate Bush taunted him for taking no position, for abandoning earlier views, and for bowing to organized labor. Accordingly, after two months of silence on the matter, Clinton announced at the beginning of October that he favored the pact. He tempered this favorability with a promise to do more to protect working conditions and the environment, along with providing more funds for adjustment benefits, but he asserted that these could be accomplished without reopening formal negotiations.

A confrontation with the issue was otherwise destined to wait for some time. The new Clinton administration moved to other matters, especially economic stimulus and deficit reduction. In March, the special trade representative, Mickey Kantor, turned to negotiating new "supplemental agreements" with Canada and Mexico, over issues of labor law and environmental regulation. Negotiations over these supplemental agreements would continue into August, and serious politicking over implementation of NAFTA would thus not really occur until after the summer congressional recess. This timing had the advantage of not conflating deficit politics, where the president was seeking a pure party-line vote in Congress, with trade politics, where he might have to rely on the congressional *Republican* Party.

By then, however, a final round of trade politics was to be additionally, institutionally complicated. For on 30 June, the U.S. Federal District Court for Washington, D.C., delivered an opinion that NAFTA required a full review of environmental impacts, potentially a six-month task in its own right. As a result, the crucial round of politicking over passage of NAFTA would occur after the summer recess, in three separate but related theaters:

❐ It would now have to occur in the courts, where the administration sought to overturn the district court ruling.

❑ It would occur in the "court of public opinion," where the administration would battle, most especially, with its old nemesis, Ross Perot, in order to create some public groundswell for NAFTA, or at least to provide "cover" for pro-NAFTA congressmen.

❑ And it would occur within Congress, where the maneuvering involved bicameral procedural gambits, programmatic compromises to expand the supportive coalition, and individual deals —often on extraneous matters—toward the same end.

In mid-August, Kantor announced that supplemental accords had indeed been completed with Mexico and Canada, institutionalizing concern for workers rights and the environment. In mid-September, on the other hand, with Congress back in session, Democratic Party leadership began to crumble. David Bonior (D–Mich.), majority whip in the House, came out formally against the pact. The White House responded by creating a special extramural lobbying team, including William Daley, a Chicago lawyer with good labor ties, and Bill Frenzel, former Republican minority whip.

Despite their efforts, in late September, Richard Gephardt (D–Mo.), majority leader in the House and long-time spokesman for efforts to restructure NAFTA, came out against it as well. Given these divisions, Thomas Foley, the Speaker of the House, was effectively neutralized. The administration regained some ground in a difficult fight, when the U.S. Court of Appeals for the District of Columbia ruled on 24 September that an environmental impact statement was not necessary for NAFTA, moving the crucial debate back into more overtly public theaters.

The opposition in public debate had already come to center on Ross Perot, running nationally televised advertisements and conducting a national speaking tour in conjunction with his new book, *Save Your Job, Save Our Country: Why NAFTA Must be Stopped—Now!* In response, the White House added Lee Iacocca, former chairman of Chrysler Corporation, to make counter advertisements, debunking the alleged loss of jobs through free trade. The ultimate pitched battle in this part of the contest, however, was not to come until early November, just before the crucial vote in Congress, when Vice-President Gore faced Perot in a television debate on the national talk show *Larry King Live.* The press awarded the vice-president a clear victory, and polls suggested a surge in public support for NAFTA.[14]

Well before then, the crucial horse-trading in Congress had gone about as far as it could. The White House considered a variety of maneuvers to bring NAFTA up first in the more sympathetic Senate —Robert Dole, Republican minority leader, was agreeable—before concluding that all would cause more ultimate damage than benefit in the House. The administration settled for an arrangement whereby relevant congressional committees would hold "mock mark-ups," thereby delaying the date at which the bill would be officially introduced and fast-track provisions activated—a deal that actually suited both sides.

On substance, the White House offered adjustments for particular industries: a change in the manner of calculating sugar imports, a mechanism to track orange juice prices. It offered adjustments to particular social groups: public works loans to districts represented by Hispanic congressmen, an extended review (and subsequent expansion) of job retraining programs for newly unemployed workers. And it dealt with individual congressmen on even more particularistic grounds, although some share of this group was predisposed to the bill and merely prospecting for additional "sweeteners." Even then, in the week before the final and decisive vote in the House, signals on its fate remained markedly mixed. In that week, three House committees reported the bill, which could no longer be amended:

❏ Ways and Means sent it to the floor with a favorable recommendation.
❏ Energy and Commerce sent it to the floor *without* a recommendation.
❏ Banking and Currency sent it to the floor with an *un*favorable recommendation.

In the event, the result was a narrow but solid victory in the House, 234–200, presaging a more substantial win in the Senate, 61–38. Given the intensity of the politicking beforehand, this immediate outcome became the story of the moment, though many analysts had already concluded that symbolism had far outrun substance for this particular program. By hindsight, most of the noteworthy aspects of the outcome sprang from its role as one more incarnation of an underlying (and continuing) policy coalition, of a social coalition in a major policy realm, demanding—and getting—an altered party alliance.

For in fact there was little difference in the outcome on NAFTA and the outcome on the *Gulf War,* two and one-half years later. The rhetoric of the debate would never have suggested such a parallel, centering, as it did on jobs and their fate. And indeed, NAFTA did engage focused economic interests in some states, sufficient to pull them from their cultural/national moorings. South Carolina Republicans thus joined national Democrats in voting no; Washington Democrats joined national Republicans (and the president) in voting yes.

Nevertheless, overall, the issue did not become an economic/welfare concern but remained in effect a cultural/national matter. As a result, NAFTA came in the end to resemble not deficit reduction, but the Gulf. In each case, the ultimate majority had been registered through a complex but still straightforward and reliable partisan coalition: an overwhelming majority of Republicans had joined with a solid majority of southern Democrats to defeat an overwhelming majority of northern Democrats. The battle over NAFTA did call into question, as never before in the postwar years, the reliability of *public* support for the concept of free trade. But in 1993 the party alliances that had long grouped this issue with foreign affairs remained sufficiently resilient to keep it lodged—firmly—there.

The filip on this—one that was familiar in American politics but nearly unprecedented elsewhere—was the relationship of the party of the president to the congressional outcome. For a *Democratic* president had managed to win by carrying an overwhelming majority of the opposition party and a solid majority of the perennially dissident faction of his own, while *losing* a majority of his party as a whole and an overwhelming majority of the dominant tendency within it. Yet the parallel outcome in 1991, on the Gulf War during the Bush presidency, was really no less remarkable. There, a president from the *minority* party—in the nation, but especially in Congress—had been opposed by a majority of the majority party and a heavy majority of its dominant tendency, and had yet managed to win, in essentially the same way.

Conclusions

A different way to summarize the situation—for the budget fiasco of 1990, the decision to go to war in the Gulf, the budget redux in 1993, and the passage of NAFTA in what might yet be a last hurrah—is just to say that all of them together reflected the ongoing contours of modern American politics. In other words, consistent across them was an underlying set of social coalitions, congealed around a continuing set of substantive concerns, as mobilized (but also strongly shaped) by a continuing party system. There continued to be cross-cutting majorities on the basic underlying issues of social welfare and cultural values. But these were cross-cutting, in essence, because the political parties did not—or perhaps could not?—offer a policy program that would "realign" the underlying social coalitions.

Which is to say that there was, in all this, nothing *inherently* "cross-cutting" about the substance of the issues themselves, and thus no automatic need for the cross-cutting majorities that their underlying social coalitions embodied. Hostility to tax increases did not logically impel the use of force in the Gulf; an emphasis on deficit reduction did not logically impel a trade agreement with Mexico. Moreover, major sections of the *mass* Democratic Party, along with major sections of the *mass* Republican Party, actually did put these issues together in *each* of the four logically possible combinations.

Nevertheless, what also existed, in terms that were practical and not hypothetical, were two ongoing policy menus: liberal welfare policies and progressive cultural policies from the national Democratic Party, along with conservative welfare policies and traditionalist cultural policies from the national Republican Party—in the face of a set of public preferences that did not coincide with either. The necessary result was some pattern of *differing* party alliances, reshuffling various factions so as to realize long-standing public majorities, but perhaps also institutionalizing the outcome even as those majorities had begun to move.

And this brings the analysis back, at last, to the key dissident group at every stage of this process, and thus to the title of the chapter. For there was, throughout, one party faction actually embodying these larger national preferences, a faction moderately supportive of social welfare but concerned about paying its bills, a faction reliably supportive of international activism but concerned about ensuring success, a faction deeply traditionalistic on cultural values in a world where economic development was putting inevitable stresses on them. By definition, then, this faction was crucial to constructing the differentiated party alliances that were perhaps the most striking aspect of politics in this period.

It was, of course, the southern Democrats, and their fate mirrors, in reverse, the entire rest of the account. For it was in the period when the issue tensions of what became the era of divided government were at their least intense, in the immediate postwar years, that the southern Democrats were at their full complement. In 1946, the year of the first postwar congressional election, there were 105 congressional seats in the Old South, breaking down into 103 Democrats and 2 Republicans, along with 22 Senate seats, yielding 22 Democrats and 0 Republicans. A half-century later, heading into the 1996 presidential elections, there were 125 congressional seats in this former Confederacy, breaking down into 61 Democrats and 64 Republicans, along with the same 22 Senate seats, now yielding 9 Democrats and 13 Republicans.

Even this understates the scope of the change. For among these formalistic modern southern Democrats are a number of individuals who are, in fact and self-consciously, orthodox "northern Democrats" instead. It would bias the argument too much to take them out of these numbers based on their policy preferences: a certain heterogeneity always marked the southern Democrats, almost by definition. But if the same numbers are calculated minus black Democrats from the South—congressmen who normally, by ideology and intention, repudiate the "southern Democratic" tag—the situation becomes more self-evidently extreme. For there is now a total population of 109 congressional seats (after removing those 16 black Democrats), for whom the remaining partisan balance is 45 Democrats and 64 Republicans. Said differently, what would have been the 103 formalistically "southern" Democrats in 1946 had become 45 by 1994—3 of whom were to switch party allegiance during 1995.

There is a further surface irony in this, of course. A national politics coming to center on the fundamental issue combination that had originally made the southern Democrats deviant, namely, liberal on social welfare but conservative on cultural values, was coinciding with the *demise* of the southern Democrats as a party faction. Yet this should probably not be treated as an irony at all. For if the rest of the nation now finds itself in the same position that southern voters once did—preferring cautious liberals on social welfare, cautious conservatives on cultural values—then there is no real basis for such a "faction" to exist. We are all southern Democrats now.

Notes

1. See, most helpfully, James L. Sundquist, *Dynamics of the Party System: Alignment and Realignment of Political Parties in the United States* (Washington, D.C.: Brookings Institution, 1973), chaps. 10–12; and Everett Carll Ladd Jr., with Charles D. Hadley, *Transformations of the American Party System* (New York: Norton, 1975), chaps. 1–2.

2. The standard sources are still the best: Angus Campbell, Philip E. Converse, Warren E. Miller, and Donald E. Stokes, *The American Voter* (New York: Wiley, 1960); and Campbell, Converse, Miller, and Stokes, *Elections and the Political Order* (New York: Wiley, 1966).

3. For the overarching framework, see Everett Carll Ladd Jr. and Charles D. Hadley, *Political Parties and Political Issues: Patterns of Political Differentiation since the New Deal* (Beverly Hills, Calif.: Sage, 1973); and Byron E. Shafer and William J.M. Claggett, *The Two Majorities: The Issue Context of Modern American Politics* (Baltimore: Johns Hopkins University Press, 1995).

4. Key sources include James Q. Wilson, *The Amateur Democrat: Club Politics in Three Cities* (Chicago: University of Chicago Press, 1963); Alan Ware, *The Breakdown of Democratic Party Organization, 1940–1980* (Oxford: Oxford University Press, 1985); and, of course, James Q. Wilson, *Political Organizations* (New York: Basic Books, 1973), esp. chap. 6.

5. This argument is elaborated in Byron E. Shafer, "The United States," in *Postwar Politics in the G-7: Orders and Eras in Comparative Perspective,* ed. Byron E. Shafer (Madison: University of Wisconsin Press, 1996), chap. 2.

6. Jean Bethke Elshtain, "Issues and Themes in the 1988 Campaign," in *The Elections of 1988,* ed. Michael Nelson (Washington, D.C.: CQ Press, 1989), chap. 5; Everett Carll Ladd Jr., "The 1988 Elections: Continuation of the Post–New Deal System," *Political Science Quarterly* 104 (Spring 1989): 1–18.

7. The best source to follow the institutional politics for the 1990 budget crisis is *Congressional Quarterly Weekly Report (CQWR),* week by week. But see, especially, Ronald D. Elving, "GOP Candidates Scrambling After Bush Tax Reversal," *CQWR,* 30 June 1990, 2033–36; Susan F. Rasky, "Accord to Reduce Spending and Raise Taxes Is Reached; Many in Congress Critical," and David E. Rosenbaum, "And the Victor Is: Bush?" *New York Times,* 1 October 1990, A1 ff.; George Hayer, "Defiant House Rebukes Bush; New Round of Fights Begins," *CQWR,* 6 October 1990, 3183–88; George Hayer, "Parties Angling for Advantage as White House Falters," *CQWR,* 13 October 1950, 3391–98; and George Hayer, "One Outcome of Budget Package: Higher Deficits on Way," *CQWR,* 3 November 1990, 3710–13.

8. On the midterm election itself, see Phil Duncan, "Budget May Shift Advantage in Congress' Closest Races," *CQWR,* 13 October 1990, 3279–83; Chuck Alson, "Warning Shots Fired by Voters More Mood Than Mandate," *CQWR,* 10 November 1990, 3896–958. For a summary of partisan standing on foreign affairs during the postwar years, see Nelson W. Polsby and Aaron Wildavsky, "Domestic Issues, Foreign Issues," in *Presidential Elections: Contemporary Strategies of American Electoral Politics,* 8th ed. (New York: Free Press, 1991), 232–35.

9. The simplest way to follow the chronology is through the *New York Times (NYT),* from 3 August 1990 through early March 1991. But see, in particular, R.W. Apple Jr., "Invading Iraqis Seize Kuwait and Its Oil; U.S. Condemns Attack, Urges United Action," *NYT,* 3 August 1990, A1; Michael R.

Gordon, "Bush Sends New Units to Gulf to Provide 'Offensive' Option; U.S. Forces Could Reach 380,000," *NYT*, 9 November 1990, A1; Special Report, "Deciding on War," *CQWR*, 5 January 1991, 7–44; Andrew Rosenthal, "Bush Halts Offensive Combat; Kuwait Freed, Iraqis Crushed," *NYT*, 28 February 1991, A1; and Rhodes Cook, "Bush's Gulf Triumph Stifles Talk of GOP Primary Challengers," *CQWR*, 9 March 1991, 581–87.

10. Gerald M. Pomper, "The Presidential Election," in *The Election of 1992*, ed. Gerald M. Pomper (Chatham, N.J.: Chatham House, 1993), chap. 5; Paul R. Abramson, John H. Aldrich, and David W. Rohde, *Change and Continuity in the 1992 Elections* (Washington, D.C.: CQ Press, 1994), chaps. 6–7.

11. Useful overview pieces include Mike Mills, "Road Work Ahead? As Economy Rallies, Clinton Must Decide Whether Quick Stimulus Is Still in Order," *CQWR*, 19 December 1992, 3884–89; Special Report, "Clinton's Bold Gamble," *CQWR*, 20 February 1993, 355–86; Special Report, "The Clinton Budget: White House Faces Reconciling Its Goals with What Congress Is Willing to Give," *CQWR*, 10 April 1993, 885–904; Special Report, "The Angst of Victory," *CQWR*, 7 August 1993, 2122–42.

12. *Congressional Quarterly Weekly Report*, whose own prior commentary had moved from surprise through irony, came to rest at the appropriate (familiar) point: "If the 1993 budget deal looks a lot like the 1990 deal, it is not by accident. Both were brokered by Democratic Congresses that had few options when they sought ways to balance the budget.

"Both packages contain sharply higher taxes on the wealthy, a nickel or less per gallon increase in the gasoline tax, deep cutbacks to Medicare providers but few or no new burdens on Medicare beneficiaries, sharp cuts in defense spending, and, amid all the deficit reduction, some social spending—chiefly an increase in the earned-income tax credit (EITC) for the working poor.

"Both packages also are initially identical in size." George Hayer, "1993 Deal: Remembrance of Things Past," *CQWR*, 7 August 1993, 2130.

13. Key overview pieces include David S. Cloud, "The NAFTA Fix: Squeezed by Democrats and Other Allies, Clinton Inherits Mexican Trade Deal," *CQWR*, 28 November 1992, 3710–13; David S. Cloud, "Sorting Out NAFTA: Rhetoric and Hyperbole on Trade Accord Cloud Debate over Pros and Cons," *CQWR*, 15 October 1993, 2791–96; Special Report, "NAFTA Crucible: Undecided Members Weigh Voter Fears as Trade Pact Showdown Approaches," *CQWR*, 6 November 1993, 3011–22; David S. Cloud, "Free Trade Ethos: Clinton Forges New Coalition to Expand Nation's Commitment to Open Markets," *CQWR*, 20 November 1993, 3174–85.

14. Phil Duncan, "Perot Gores His Own Ox," *CQWR*, 13 November 1993, 3105. The Perot book was Ross Perot with Pat Choate, *Save Your Job, Save Our Country: Why NAFTA Must Be Stopped—Now!* (New York: Hyperion, 1993).

Index

Abortion, as issue, 90, 93, 94, 108
Affirmative action, 94, 98
African Americans, and Democratic affiliation, 100, 101, 102, 121
See also Blacks
"Alienation," of 1960s, 39–40
American politics
forces governing, 136–39
as moralized, 141–42
See also Budgetary politics; Cultural politics; Politics
American South
economic/political shifts in, 153–54
and New Deal, 149
See also Southern whites
"Americorps," 65
Antipartyism, 16, 20
Authority
deference to, 75, 76, 80
erosion of, 84
suspicion of, 85

Baby-boom generation, ideology of, 85–86
Ballot, role of, 52
Begala, Paul, 67
Big business, 35
corruption of, 38–39
Big government, corruption of, 39–40
See also Government
Big labor, corruption of, 39
See also Labor

Blacks
cultural attitudes of, 108, 109, 118, 119
and Democratic affiliation, 92, 100, 121
racial attitude of, 115, 116
white hunger for success of, 138
See also African Americans
Blue-collar coalition, 148
Bonior, David, 170
Bryan, William Jennings, 37
Bryanites, challenge of, 17
BTU tax, 166
Buchanan, Pat, 93
Budgetary politics, in 1990, 155–58
See also American politics; Cultural politics; Politics
Burnham, Walter Dean, 3
Burns, James MacGregor, 19, 27n. 20
Bush, George, 41, 42, 53, 62, 68, 164
election of, 156
and GATT, 168
and Gulf War, 159
popularity of, 161
Butler, Harold, 32, 44

Calhoun, John C., 8
Cambreleng, Churchill, 12–13
Canada, free-trade pact with, 168
Capone, Al, 79
Carter, Jimmy, 40, 41, 60

Carville, James, 41
Catholics
and abortion, 108
cultural attitudes of, 108, 109, 118, 119
as Democrats, 100, 101, 102, 121
racial attitudes of, 115, 116
Chicago City Council, 75–76
Chicago Tribune, 78
China, fall of, to communists, 36
Christian Coalition, 137
See also Christian Right
Christian Right, 98, 137
Civic culture, polarizing, coarsening of, 6
Civil rights
bills for, 35–36, 40
Republican Party and, 115, 118
revolution in, 141, 143
Civil Rights Act of 1964, 92, 138
Civil rights movement, 92
Democratic Party and, 100, 115
pace of, 94
Cleavage(s)
issue-based, 104–11
social welfare, 100, 104
Clinton, Bill, 36, 41, 53
campaign strategy of, 168–69
campaign style of, 64–65
limitations of, 64

About the Authors

BYRON E. SHAFER is Andrew W. Mellon Professor of American Government at Oxford University and a Professorial Fellow in Politics at Nuffield College. His publications include *The Two Majorities: The Issue Context of Modern American Politics* (with William Claggett); *Bifurcated Politics: Evolution and Reform in the National Party Convention*; and *Quiet Revolution: The Struggle for the Democratic Party and the Shaping of Post-Reform Politics*.

JOEL H. SILBEY is President White Professor of History at Cornell University. He is the editor-in-chief of the *Encyclopedia of the American Legislative System*, and his publications include *The American Political Nation, 1838–1893; A Respectable Minority: The Democratic Party in the Civil War Era, 1860–1868*; and *The Partisan Imperative: The Dynamics of American Politics before the Civil War*.

MICHAEL BARONE is Senior Writer and Political Columnist at *U.S. News & World Report*. His publications include *Our Country: The Shaping of America from Roosevelt to Reagan* and *The Almanac of American Politics* (with Grant Ujifusa), which has been published biennially for many years.

CHARLES O. JONES is Glenn B. and Cleone Orr Harkins Professor of Political Science at the University of Wisconsin, Madison. He is a past president of the American Political Science Association and past editor of the *American Political Science Review*. His publications include *The Presidency in a Separated System; The Trusteeship Presidency: Jimmy Carter and the U.S. Congress*; and *Clean Air: The Policies and Politics of Pollution Control*.

ALAN EHRENHALT is executive editor of *Governing: The States and Localities*. His publications include *The United States of Ambition: Politicians, Power, and the Pursuit of Office* and *The Lost City:*

Discovering the Forgotten Virtues of Community in the Chicago of the 1950s.

EDWARD G. CARMINES is Rudy Professor of Political Science and chairman of the Political Science Department at Indiana University. His publications include *Issue Evolution: Race and the Transformation of American Politics* (with James A. Stimson) and *The Power of Justice: Liberalism and a New Politics of Race* (with Paul M. Sniderman).

GEOFFREY C. LAYMAN is assistant professor of political science at Vanderbilt University. He received his Ph.D. from Indiana University. Professor Layman won the American Political Science Association's Aaron Wildavsky Memorial Award for the Best Dissertation in Religion and Politics in 1995–96 for his "Parties and Culture Wars: The Manifestation of Cultural Conflict in the American Party System."

THOMAS B. EDSALL is a national political reporter for the *Washington Post*. His publications include *Chain Reaction: The Impact of Race, Rights, and Taxes on American Politics* (with Mary D. Edsall); *Power and Money;* and *The New Politics of Inequality.*